W9-DHK-376

Ready, Set, Run!

A Student Guide to SAS® Software for Microsoft® Windows®

Daniel T. Larose • Chun Jin
Central Connecticut State University

WITHDRAWN

Mayfield Publishing Company
Mountain View, California
London • Toronto

243313

DEC 0 7 2000

To Debra, Irene, Chantal, and Ellyriane
And to Xiaoyan and Daniel

Copyright © 1998 by Mayfield Publishing Company

All rights reserved. No portion of this book may be reproduced in any form or by any means without written permission of the publisher.

Library of Congress Cataloging-in-Publication Data

Larose, Daniel T.
   Ready, set, run! : a student guide to SAS software for microsoft windows / Daniel T. Larose, Chun Jin.
       p.   cm.
   Includes bibliographical references.
   ISBN 0-7674-0422-X
   1. SAS (Computer file)   2. Microsoft Windows (Computer file)
I. Jin, Chun.   II. Title.
QA276.4.L37   1998   97-43412
519.5'0285'5369—DC21   CIP

SAS is a registered trademark of SAS Institute, Inc., Cary, NC, USA.
SAS System output is printed with permission of SAS Institute, Inc., Cary, NC, USA.
Windows® is a registered trademark of Microsoft Corporation.

Manufactured in the United States of America
10   9   8   7   6   5   4   3   2   1

Mayfield Publishing Company
1280 Villa Street
Mountain View, California, 94041

Sponsoring editor, Franklin C. Graham; production editor, Lynn Rabin Bauer; manuscript editor, Tom Briggs; design manager, Susan Breitbard; cover designer, Jean Mailander; cover photograph, © Alán Gallegos/AG Photograph; manufacturing manager, Randy Hurst. The text was set in 11/14 Times Roman by Archetype Book Composition and printed on 50# Thor Offset by Malloy Lithographing.

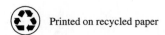 Printed on recycled paper

Preface

This handbook furnishes the basic information needed to use SAS® Software for Microsoft® Windows®. SAS software is perhaps the most powerful statistical computing package in the world, and SAS for Windows gives beginning statistics students an opportunity to tap into this power.

As an adjunct to the primary textbook for an introductory statistics or research methods course, this handbook is a user-friendly instrument for merging modern computational methods into such a course.

SAS software is widely used in government, the pharmaceutical industry, the behavioral sciences and many other areas. Instructors wishing to provide their students with real-world skills may thus require experience with SAS software, as does the mathematics department at our university. However, the dearth of clear and easily understandable student guides for SAS for Windows led us to develop our own pedagogical materials. This handbook grew out of these materials and out of our desire to provide up-to-date access for our own students to the most intuitive platform (Microsoft® Windows®) for the most powerful statistical package (SAS software). SAS for Windows may be used with Windows 3.1®, Windows 95®, or Windows NT®.

The book is intended for students (mostly nonstatistics majors) who may require a gentle introduction to the computational side of statistics. It is written at a level that any college student (first year and up) should find completely accessible. It delivers crystal clear, step-by-step instructions, with generous doses of screen-shot illustrations to guide users through what may be their first computer experience. In fact, *we assume no previous computer experience at all.*

The handbook consists of 10 topical assignments, in which students learn how to merge their statistical knowledge with new computational techniques. Each assignment begins with an outline of the objectives: What will students learn in this assignment? The topics range from the basics of SAS software through regression and Chi-square analysis. Each topic is introduced by way of an example, and the sample SAS commands are explained in clear, step-by-step instructions. The resulting output is discussed in detail, with emphasis on interpretation of the results. The instructions are illustrated by plentiful screen shots of SAS for Windows to help students visualize their progress. Finally, each assignment ends with an opportunity for students to increase their computational competence by performing these tasks.

The assignments are arranged by topic, paralleling most of the concepts covered in a typical introductory statistics course. Assignment 1 introduces the basics of SAS software—how to use SAS for Windows, how to type in a SAS program, how to check for errors, how to save the program, and how to print out the results. Assignment 2 introduces students to numerical descriptive measures, while Assignment 3 examines graphical descriptive methods such as plots. SAS for Windows has very-high-resolution graphics capability. Both assignments are written in the spirit of exploratory data analysis. In fact, throughout the handbook, students are encouraged to explore the data before analysis, rather than simply reporting the results. The t tests are examined in Assignment 4 (one-sample t test) and Assignment 5 (two-sample t tests). Analysis of variance (ANOVA) is covered in Assignment 6 (one-way ANOVA) and Assignment 7 (two-way ANOVA). Correlation between two variables is discussed in Assignment 8, while simple linear regression is introduced in Assignment 9. Finally, Assignment 10 examines Chi-square analysis.

Most of the examples used in the handbook come from *Statistics for the Behavioral Sciences,* Second Edition, by B. Michael Thorne and Steve Slane, published by Mayfield. This handbook is intended as a sister publication to *Ready, Set, Go! A Student Guide to SPSS® for Windows 7.5®,* by Thomas W. Pavkov and Kent A. Pierce, also published by Mayfield. The instructor thus has a choice of software guides to complement the course.

ACKNOWLEDGMENTS

We are happy to acknowledge the people at Mayfield Publishing Company for their support of this project. In particular, we would like to extend wholehearted thanks to our sponsoring editor, Franklin C. Graham, for his spirited support of the concept. We would also like to express our appreciation for our developmental editor, Susan Shook, whose many cogent suggestions greatly improved the text. Also, we are deeply grateful to our production editor, Lynn Rabin Bauer, for her enthusiastic support and to our copyeditor, Tom Briggs, for his fine work.

Finally, we would like to express our appreciation for our colleagues who reviewed the manuscript: Melvin G. Pronga (Central Connecticut State University), Daniel S. Miller (Central Connecticut State University), and Robert H. Crouse (Central Connecticut State University).

Contents

ASSIGNMENT 1

Learning the Basics of SAS for Windows

OBJECTIVES

To start SAS for Windows

To identify the elements of the SAS program

To run the SAS program

To check for errors

To view and print your results

To save your SAS program

To exit from SAS for Windows

This assignment presents step-by-step instructions for using some of the basic procedures of SAS Software for Microsoft® Windows®. For example, you will learn to start up (launch) SAS for Windows from the usual Microsoft® Windows 3.1® Program Manager screen. While accessing methods may differ from college to college, you will find that once SAS for Windows is launched, the procedures covered in this book are fairly universal. You will encounter sample screens that will guide you as you learn; these illustrations are generated from SAS for Windows Version 6.12.

Sometimes, you may encounter situations that are not covered in this book or make errors that you do not understand. If so, then refer to the troubleshooting Appendix, which gives solutions to common errors. Also, you may seek help from your instructor or a statistical consultant. Finally, resources on the World Wide Web give answers to frequently asked questions (see References).

This first assignment presents vital information on how to use SAS for Windows. You will learn what SAS for Windows is, how to launch it, what the three main windows are, how to type in a SAS program, how to run the program, how and where to check for errors, how to save the program, how to print out (get a hard or paper copy of) your program or your results, and finally, how to exit from SAS for Windows.

WHAT IS SAS FOR WINDOWS?

SAS for Windows is a software package for data analysis. Its procedures range from simple summary statistics to complex and powerful multivariate methods. The same SAS system that helps pharmaceutical companies demonstrate the safety and efficacy of new drugs can also help students uncover the exciting world of statistics.

In fact, this book is intended for students who are just starting out on their statistics journey and who may have no previous experience with computers. We emphasize that *this book assumes no previous experience with computers.* If you have little confidence in your ability to interact with computers ("I hate computers" or "Computers hate me"), then this book is for you. We will take you step-by-step, slowly and methodically, from the moment you sit in front of the machine until the proud moment when you print out your results.

If you are proficient at Windows® but have no knowledge of SAS software, then this book will open the world of statistical computing in the Windows® environment. If you have experience only with mainframe SAS applications, then this book is a gentle introduction to the Windows® version, which loses nothing in power while gaining significantly in user-friendliness.

STARTING SAS FOR WINDOWS

Windows® is a graphical user interface that greatly facilitates the use of computer software. When you launch Windows 3.1®, the first window to appear is the Program Manager (Figure 1.1).

In many microcomputer labs, this is the screen you will see when you first sit down at the computer. If you see the DOS prompt (c:\), typing in win and hitting the Enter key will often get you to the Windows® Program Manager. If there is a facility-specific menu interface, ask the lab assistant how to get to the Windows® Program Manager.

The Program Manager screen shows the collection of applications that can be used on your computer. Figure 1.1 is only an example; your Program Manager will probably look different because your computer has different software than ours. You will be using the *mouse* (palm-sized device with two buttons) as a pointing-and-clicking device to tell the computer what to do. The pointer on the screen moves as the mouse moves. The little pictures in the Program Manager are called *icons* and represent the individual software applications on your computer.

Find the icon for SAS for Windows. It may have various names (for example, SAS System), but the term SAS should appear. Move the mouse until the pointer

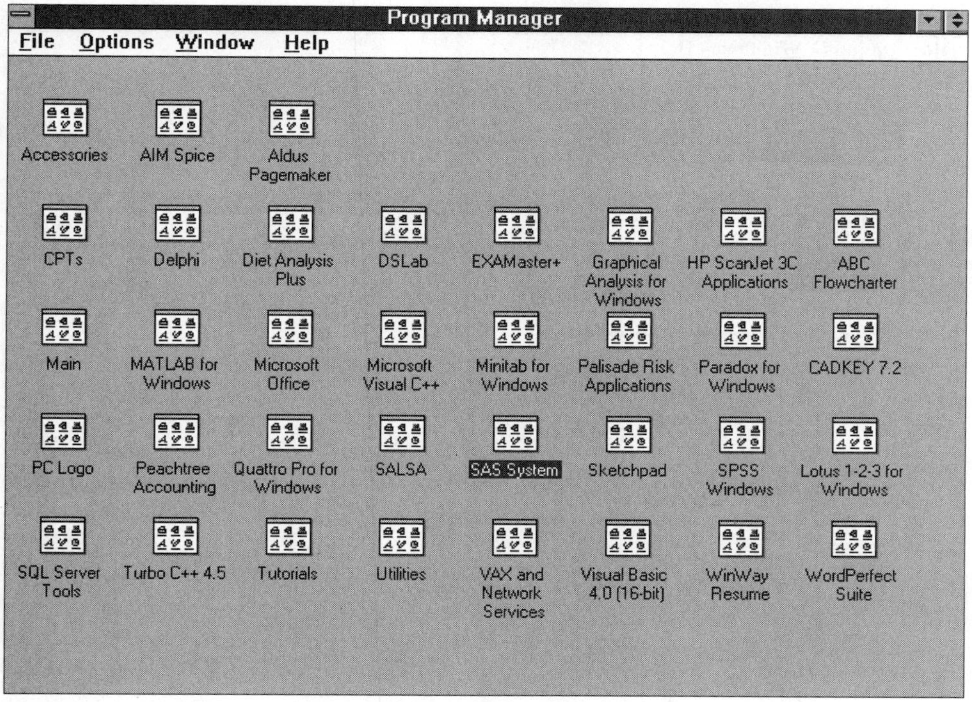

FIGURE 1.1 Finding the SAS System for Windows® Icon in the Program Manager

is over this icon, and click once. To *click* means to press and quickly release the left mouse button. To *double-click* means to do this twice in rapid succession. Clicking once (single click) on an icon will highlight the icon name, as in Figure 1.1. Now, double-click on the SAS icon. This action opens up the SAS group, a new window containing the SAS applications on your computer (Figure 1.2, p. 4).

Now, double click on the icon **The SAS System for Windows v6.12** to launch the SAS for Windows software. From time to time, your pointer will turn into an hourglass. This is the computer's way of asking you to wait while it performs a task. Its present task is loading the SAS for Windows software. When your screen looks something like Figure 1.3 (p. 5), with **SAS** in the window title at the top, you will know that you have launched SAS for Windows. Don't forget that your screen may look different, as it is unlikely that any two configurations are exactly alike.

THE THREE MAIN SAS WINDOWS

When SAS for Windows is launched, the result (see Figure 1.3) is the *SAS application workspace (SAS AWS)*. The SAS AWS consists of all open SAS windows.

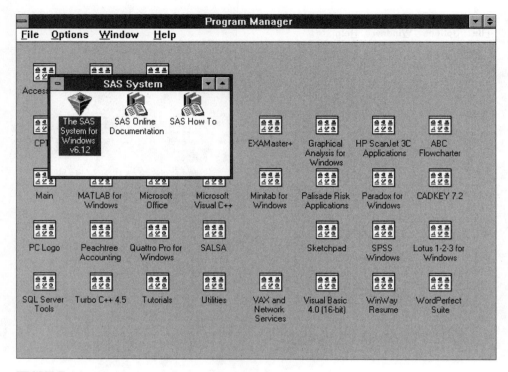

FIGURE 1.2 The SAS for Windows Program Group

Think of it as your desktop work area. The individual windows within the SAS AWS are the *child windows*. For example, in Figure 1.3, the child windows are the PROGRAM EDITOR, the LOG, the OUTPUT MANAGER, and the OUTPUT windows.

Below the AWS title SAS, you find the *menu bar* (File, Edit, View, Locals, and so on). You use the menu bar to access many different features of SAS for Windows through the use of pull-down menus, which display a range of choices (more on this later). Below the menu bar is the *toolbar,* which contains shortcuts to some of the most commonly performed tasks (more on this later as well).

Below the tool bar are the four child windows. Actually, to tidy up the AWS, we would like either to *cascade* or *tile* the child windows. To cascade the child windows, click on Window on the menu bar; a pull-down menu will appear (Figure 1.4). Now, click on Cascade. The child windows will all line up neatly behind one another, as in Figure 1.4. To tile the child windows, click on Window on the menu bar and then click on Tile. The windows will then all share equally the AWS space (Figure 1.5, p. 6). Notice in Figures 1.4 and 1.5 that the currently active window, the PROGRAM EDITOR, is highlighted.

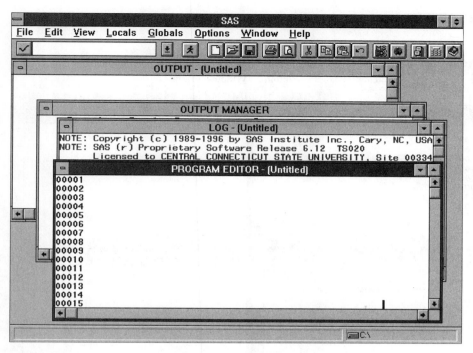

FIGURE 1.3   The SAS for Windows Application Workspace

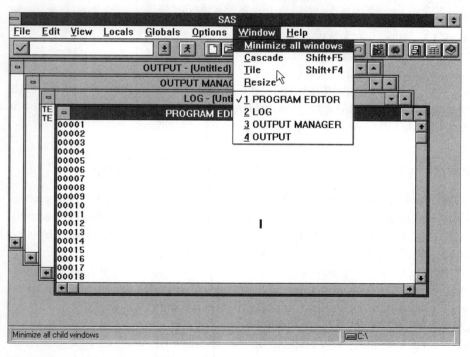

FIGURE 1.4   Cascading the Child Windows

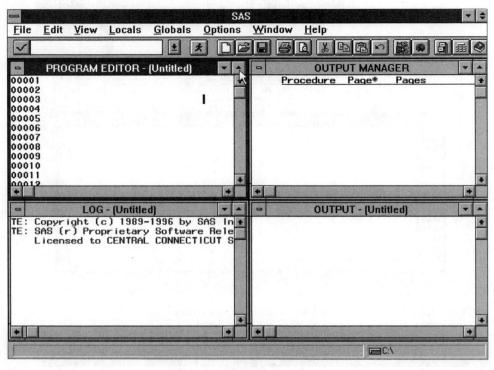

FIGURE 1.5   Tiling the Child Windows

As we proceed, we will introduce the three main child windows of the SAS software: the PROGRAM EDITOR, LOG, and OUTPUT windows. We will not discuss the OUTPUT MANAGER window in this handbook.

HOW TO TYPE IN A PROGRAM: THE PROGRAM EDITOR

SAS for Windows differs from certain other statistical software packages such as SPSS and Minitab, in that it requires you to submit a program, rather than simply choose from a menu of procedures. A *program* is simply a set of step-by-step instructions telling the SAS compiler what you would like it to do.

Here's an example of how to type in a simple SAS program. We use the PRO-GRAM EDITOR to type in these instructions (also called *SAS code*). To get a clearer view of our work, we would like to enlarge the AWS area allotted to the PROGRAM EDITOR window. We do this by maximizing the PROGRAM EDITOR window, that is, by clicking on the up-arrow in the upper-right corner of the PROGRAM EDITOR child window (see Figure 1.5). The result is shown in

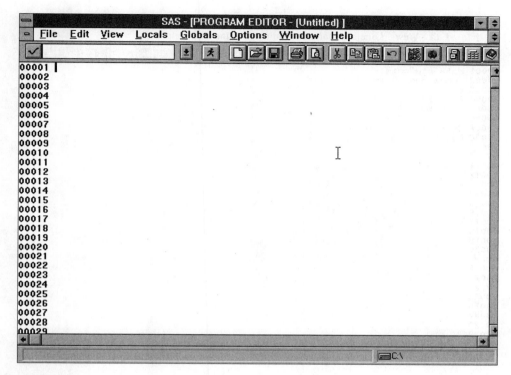

FIGURE 1.6 The SAS for Windows PROGRAM EDITOR

Figure 1.6. The PROGRAM EDITOR operates just like any simple Windows®
text editor, such as Notepad. The numbers on the left (see Figure 1.6) are line numbers and may not appear in your configuration.

THE ELEMENTS OF A SAS PROGRAM

Most SAS programs consist of two steps: DATA steps and PROC steps. The
DATA step is used to create data sets and manipulate your data. The PROC step
calls on the extensive library of SAS procedures (PROCs) to perform statistical
analyses of your chosen data set. It is important to remember that every SAS statement ends in a semicolon (;).

The DATA Step

The first SAS statement in the DATA step is the **DATA** statement.

DATA *dataname*;

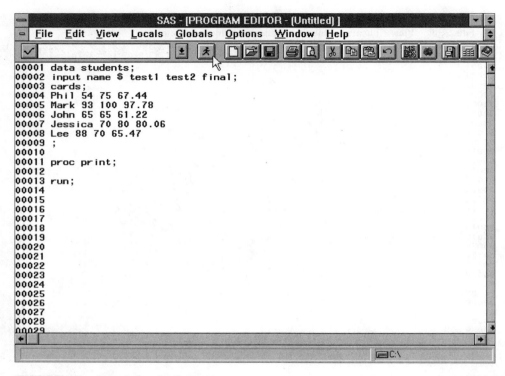

FIGURE 1.7   Submitting the Program

The word **DATA** means that you intend to read a data file and store the data in a SAS data set. Substitute the name of your data set for **dataname**, using at most eight characters.

Consider our DATA step. In our example program (Figure 1.7), we create a data set called **students** by typing in

    data students;

Our next SAS statement in the DATA step is the **INPUT** statement:

    INPUT *variable1 variable2 ... last variable;*

The **INPUT** statement tells the computer the names of the variables it is expected to read on any given line of data. Again, use at most eight characters per name.

In our example program, the variable names are **name**, **test1**, **test2**, and **final**.

    input name $ test1 test2 final;

These represent, for each student, the student's name, the scores on Test 1 and Test 2, and the final average for the course. Note the $ after the variable name, denoting this variable as qualitative (basically non-numerical) rather than quantitative (numerical). Later, we will see some other ways to input data (see the INFILE command in Assignment 3).

The next statement in the DATA step is the CARDS statement:

> cards;

We use the CARDS statement to tell the computer that the data follows immediately.

The Data Itself

Notice that our data set is entered on a student-by-student (case-by-case) basis, with one student on each line. Also note the single semicolon on a new line at the end of the data and the absence of semicolons within the data set.

> Phil 54 75 67.44
> Mark 93 100 97.78
> John 65 65 61.22
> Jessica 70 80 80.06
> Lee 88 70 65.47
> ;

The PROC Step

SAS procedures (PROCs) read the data sets, perform various manipulations and statistical analyses, and display the results of these computations in the OUTPUT window. For example, the *t* test procedure performs a *t* test on variables of interest.

> PROC *procname;*

The word *PROC* means that you wish to call on a SAS procedure. Substitute the name of the procedure you wish to invoke for procname. We will learn how to call on several different PROCs over the course of these 10 assignments.

Consider our PROC step. The only task we set for the SAS program to perform in this first example is to display the data in the OUTPUT window by calling on PROC PRINT. This use of the word *PRINT* may be misleading: PROC PRINT does not produce a hard copy, but simply displays the data in the OUTPUT window. Finally, notice the RUN command. It is good SAS form to follow every PROC by a RUN command.

HOW TO RUN THE PROGRAM

Now we have finished typing in our SAS program, but SAS for Windows hasn't performed any of the program instructions yet. To execute these instructions, we must *submit* the program. From the PROGRAM EDITOR toolbar, click on the icon of the running man (see Figure 1.7). This tells SAS for Windows to run your program. Alternatively, you can click on Locals in the menu bar and then on Submit in the pull-down menu.

WHERE TO CHECK FOR ERRORS:
THE SAS LOG

Once you have submitted your SAS program, the tiled windows will reappear, allowing you to easily choose which window you would like to work in (Figure 1.8).

At this point, we should check the LOG window to see if there are any errors or warnings from the SAS compiler regarding our program. Maximize the LOG window (see Figure 1.8 for where to click) so we can get a better view (Figure 1.9).

The LOG window is where SAS for Windows tells you about the technical side of processing your program. The blue writing lists notes, warnings, and error messages; the black writing lists each line of your program that was processed. In this example, there are no warnings or error messages. In Assignment 3, we will see an example of LOG error messages and ways to handle them.

WHERE RESULTS ARE DISPLAYED:
THE OUTPUT WINDOW

Because there were no warnings or error messages in our SAS log, we are ready to examine the output produced by the program. Click on Window and then OUTPUT. If you see a blank page, try scrolling to the right using the horizontal scrollbar at the bottom of the screen. The result is shown in Figure 1.10 (p. 12).

The OUTPUT window displays your results, such as summary statistics, graphical plots, or, in our case, a simple display of the data. You may peruse your output to see if it contains everything you want (and nothing you don't). If you are not satisfied, you can return to the PROGRAM EDITOR to change or add something to your program. To do this, click on Window and Tile, and then highlight

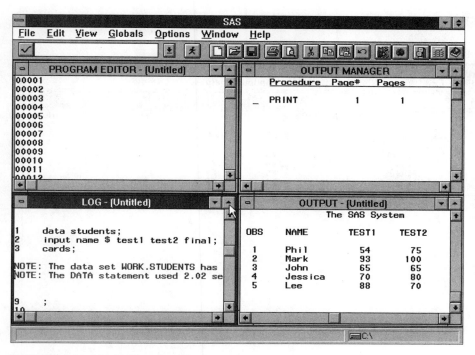

FIGURE 1.8 Maximizing the LOG Window

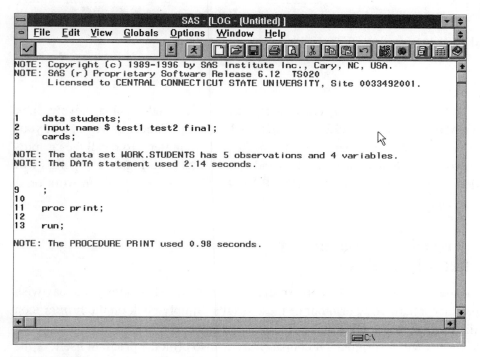

FIGURE 1.9 The LOG Window

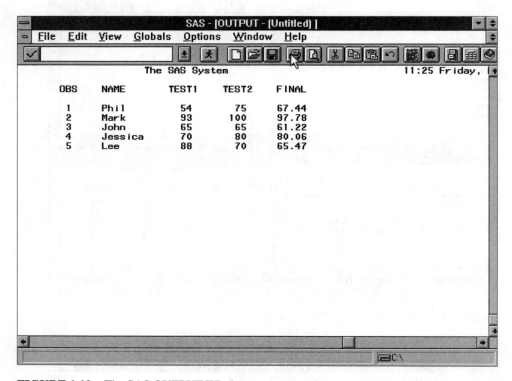

FIGURE 1.10   The SAS OUTPUT Window

the PROGRAM EDITOR by clicking anywhere on its window; alternatively, click on **Window** and then **PROGRAM EDITOR**. You will notice, however, that your program is gone (it has been submitted to the SAS compiler). To recall the last program you submitted, click on **Locals** and then **Recall text** (Figure 1.11). This will retrieve your program into the PROGRAM EDITOR so that you can work on it some more.

HOW TO PRINT YOUR RESULTS, OR PROGRAM, OR LOG

If you are happy with the results displayed in the OUTPUT window, you may wish to produce a hard-copy printout of these results. Simply click on the *printer* icon in the toolbar in the OUTPUT window (see Figure 1.10), and a paper copy of your results will be printed. Of course, you can also print the program itself, or the

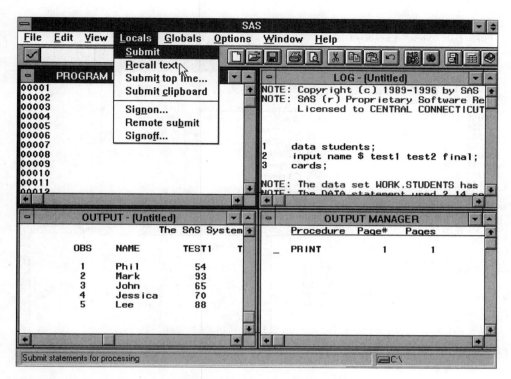

FIGURE 1.11 Retrieving Your Program into the PROGRAM EDITOR

SAS log, by highlighting the appropriate window and clicking on the printer icon as before.

HOW TO SAVE YOUR PROGRAM

To avoid having to retype the program each time you sit down at the computer, you may want to save it to disk. Generally, you can save it to two types of disk drives: the computer hard drive, often denoted as the c: drive, and a diskette drive, often denoted as the a: (or b:) drive. If the computer you are working on does not belong to you (for example, if you are in a microcomputer lab on campus), then you should not save your program on the computer's hard drive. Instead, bring a formatted diskette and save your program on the diskette.

To save your program, highlight the PROGRAM EDITOR window, and then click on File in the menu bar and Save in the pull-down menu. This displays a *dialog box,* which asks you to name your program file and to specify where you

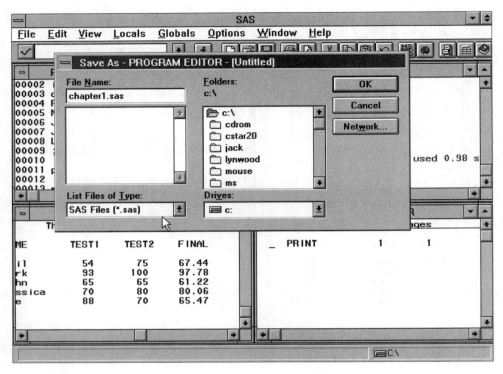

FIGURE 1.12   Saving Your Program

want to save it. Click on the box under File Name and type in chapter1.sas (Figure 1.12).

Of course, you can name your program file whatever you want, so long as you retain the file extension (.SAS) and the first part (before the .SAS) does not exceed eight characters. Under Folders, you can choose which directory to save it to. Under Drives, you can choose which drive to save it to. For example, if you need to save it on a diskette, insert the diskette, click on the down-arrow under Drives, click on a:, and then give it a filename as before. To complete the save, click on the OK button.

HOW TO EXIT THE SAS SESSION

When you are done with your work and wish to exit the SAS application, click on File in the menu bar and then Exit (Figure 1.13). This ends your SAS for Windows session and returns you to a screen similar to the one shown in Figure 1.1.

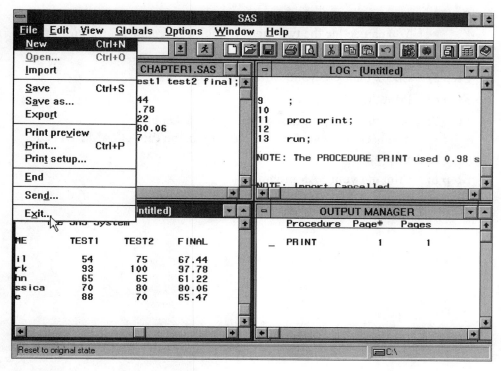

FIGURE 1.13 Exiting SAS for Windows

ON YOUR OWN

Hands-On Exercise 1: Basics of SAS for Windows

To gain some experience in using SAS for Windows, you should perform the following tasks step-by-step.

In a simple reaction-time test, a person tries to catch a ruler between thumb and forefinger after it has been released suddenly by another person. The following are scores generated with the test in a statistics class:

| Females | 5 | 13 | 7 | 9 | 9 | 9 | 2 | 5 | 6 |
| Males | 5 | 5 | 9 | 8 | 8 | 6 | 4 | 7 | 3 |

Using SAS for Windows, write a SAS program to display the given data.

Step 1: Load SAS for Windows.

Step 2: Activate the PROGRAM EDITOR window.

Step 3:   Type in a simple SAS program.

➤   You can define the two input variables as *females* and *males*.

Step 4:   Submit your SAS program to run.

Step 5:   Check the LOG window for possible errors.

Step 6:   Print the SAS output.

Step 7:   Save the SAS program on your own diskette.

➤   You need to recall the SAS program in the PROGRAM EDITOR window.

Step 8:   Print out your SAS program.

Step 9:   Exit the SAS session.

ASSIGNMENT 2

Descriptive Statistics

OBJECTIVES

To use PROC UNIVARIATE

To read and print the output from PROC UNIVARIATE

WHAT IS EXPLORATORY DATA ANALYSIS?

Now that you have gained some familiarity with the basics of SAS for Windows, it is time to do some statistical analysis. Assignment 2 covers numerical summaries of data sets, that is, descriptive statistics. Assignment 3 will focus on graphical summaries of data sets.

Before engaging in detailed data analysis, you should always *explore* the data—get an idea of where the middle of the data is, how spread out the data are, what the extremes of the data are, and what the overall shape of the data is. This is called *exploratory data analysis*.

HOW TO USE PROC UNIVARIATE TO
GENERATE DESCRIPTIVE STATISTICS

Suppose we want to explore a given data set. We might begin by providing numerical summaries of the data set. Among the many ways to accomplish this in SAS for Windows is to use PROC UNIVARIATE. The basic syntax for this procedure is

```
PROC univariate;
VAR varname;
```

These two lines of SAS code will provide a numerical summary of the quantitative variable **varname**, from the last defined data set. The summary will include measures of central tendency such as the mean and the median and measures of dispersion such as the variance and standard deviation, as well as sample size, quantiles, and many other statistics that will help describe your data set.

AN EXAMPLE USING PROC UNIVARIATE

We would like to explore a small sample data set called **years**, consisting of the ages in years of 20 young people. Let's write a simple SAS program using PROC UNIVARIATE.

Click on **Window** in the menu bar and then **PROGRAM EDITOR** in the pull-down menu. For convenience, we will begin using the shorthand notation "Click on **Window/PROGRAM EDITOR**" to denote these instructions. If some other program is already there, click on **Edit/Clear text**.

Then type in the following short program (Figure 2.1):

```
data years;
input age @@;
cards;

15 12 9 10 5 12 3 7 16 12
14 11 8 7 4 18 19 6 8 14
;

proc print;
run;

proc univariate;
var age;
run;
```

The first statement in the DATA step is the **DATA** statement, which defines a SAS data set called **years**. The **INPUT** statement specifies the name of the variables in the data set; here, we have only one variable, **age**. Note the @@ notation in the **INPUT** statement. This informs the computer that more than one set of variable values will be input on a single line. Without the @@ notation, the software would expect a new line for each new set of variable values. The data set follows the **CARDS** statement, as in Assignment 1.

Other ways of accessing data include reading a remote data file using the **INFILE** command (as we will see in Assignment 3). PROC PRINT writes the data to the OUTPUT window, as we saw in Assignment 1.

Finally, PROC UNIVARIATE will provide us with the numerical summaries we need to explore our sample data set **years**. The variable of interest is **age** (later, for example in Assignment 3, we will have more than one variable in the data set). Once you type in the program, submit it by clicking on the running man icon (see Figure 2.1).

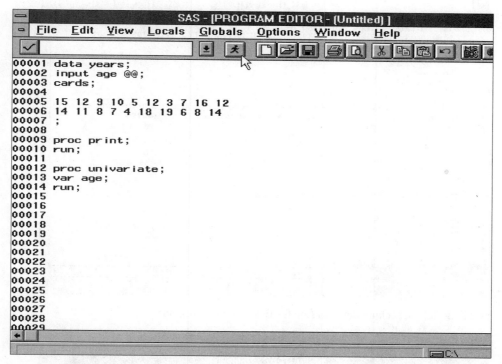

FIGURE 2.1   The Program for Descriptive Statistics

Always check the SAS log file for errors by clicking on Window/LOG (Figure 2.2). If there is no LOG in the Window menu, click on Globals/LOG. Figure 2.2 shows no errors or warnings in the SAS log, so proceed to the output by clicking on Window/OUTPUT.

The first "page" of the output (Figure 2.3) shows the results of PROC PRINT, a simple list of the variable values for each observation. Scroll down (see the pointer in Figure 2.3) until you arrive at the second "page" of the output (Figure 2.4). Here is a wealth of numerical information that nicely summarizes the data set years.

The sample size n is 20. The mean age $\overline{X}$ is 10.5, with a standard deviation S of 4.582576. There are many other statistics, such as skewness and kurtosis, that your instructor may not be using at this point. On the right (to get a better look, scroll to the right on the horizontal scrollbar) are located more descriptive statistics, including the quantiles, the median (10.5), the range (16), and the mode (12).

If you want to print out the results, click on the printer icon (see Figure 2.4).

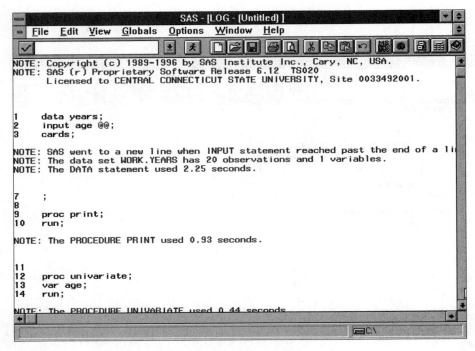

FIGURE 2.2 Checking the SAS Log for Errors in Our Program

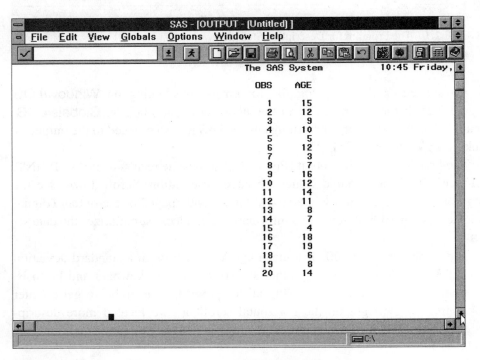

FIGURE 2.3 The First Page of Output from PROC PRINT

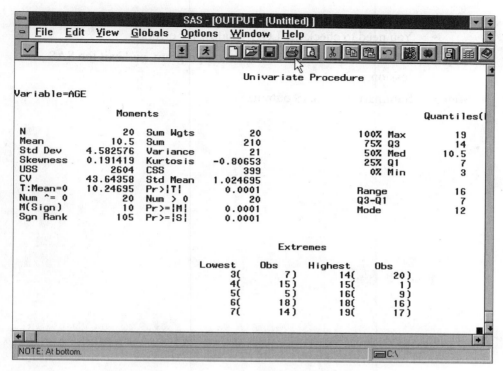

FIGURE 2.4 The Second Page of Output from PROC UNIVARIATE

ON YOUR OWN

Hands-On Exercise 2: Descriptive Statistics

To get more experience in obtaining the numerical summary of a data set, you should perform the following tasks step-by-step.

In a study of problem solving, we have measured the number of "brainteasers" correctly solved in 10 minutes by a group of 10 students. Here are the scores:

    2   0   6   5   5   1   7   4   4   6

Using SAS for Windows, write a SAS program using PROC UNIVARIATE to obtain the numerical summary of the given data set.

Step 1: Load the SAS software, and activate the PROGRAM EDITOR window.

Step 2: Type in a simple SAS program, and use PROC UNIVARIATE in your program.

Step 3: Submit the SAS program to run.
➤ You need to check the LOG window for errors.

Step 4: Print the SAS output, save the SAS program, and exit the SAS session.

Step 5: Summarize the SAS output.

ASSIGNMENT 3

Making a Graphic

OBJECTIVES

To load data or a program from a diskette

To create text-based graphics

To handle program errors using SAS log

To preview your output

To create high-resolution graphics

In Assignment 2, we learned how to produce numerical descriptive summaries of the data using PROC UNIVARIATE. Sometimes, however, pictures tell a fuller story about the data. Therefore, in this assignment, we will discuss how to create these pictures, or graphical representations of the data. Specifically, you will learn how to load data (or a program) from a diskette, how to create text-based graphics, how to handle program errors using SAS log, how to preview your output before printing, and how to create and print high-resolution graphics.

LOADING DATA OR A PROGRAM FROM A DISKETTE

Diskettes are portable storage media that can contain data, SAS programs, or other computer files. Because students often are required to analyze data that are stored on a diskette, it is important to learn how to get the data (or program) from the diskette into the SAS for Windows system.

Assume that our datafile is on a diskette, which has been inserted into the proper disk drive (usually a:). The first step is to open the file. Click on the *open file folder* icon in the toolbar (Figure 3.1). A dialog box will appear (the contents will be different for your computer), and we need to select the a: drive, which houses the diskette. Under Drives, click on the down-arrow and on the a: drive. Then, under List Files of Type, again click on the down-arrow (Figure 3.2) and All Files (*.*). This directs the computer to list all files on your diskette. You should see the drive light illuminated, and you might hear the soft grinding of the

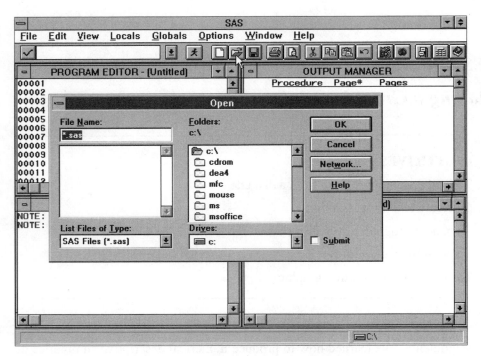

FIGURE 3.1   Step 1 of Opening a File: The Dialog Box for Opening a File

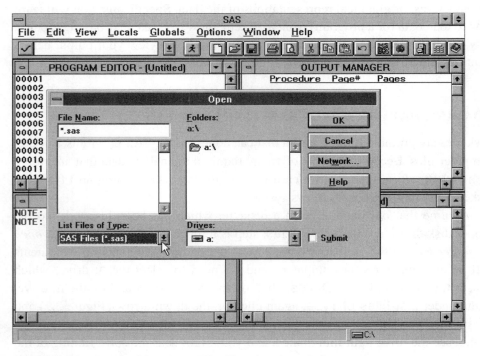

FIGURE 3.2   Step 2 of Opening a File: Choosing the a: Drive

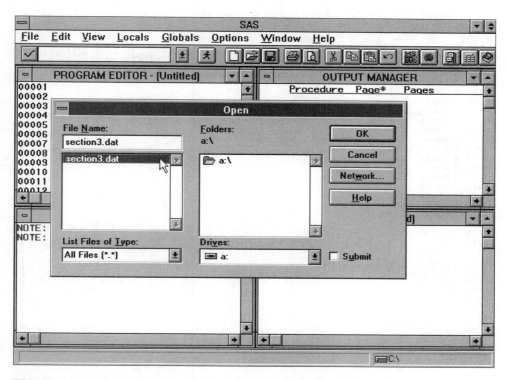

FIGURE 3.3   Step 3 of Opening a File: Selecting the File You Wish to Open

a: drive as the diskette inside it is searched for files. The result will look something like Figure 3.3; again, the files on your diskette will differ from those on ours.

Now locate the datafile you wish to open. The datafile we will use for this assignment is called section3.dat. The .dat is the filename extension indicating that this is a datafile. Click on your filename, and on the OK button to load the datafile into the PROGRAM EDITOR window (Figure 3.4). Notice the name of the file, section3.dat, in the title bar at the top of Figure 3.4.

Now we can write our SAS program by typing commands in the PROGRAM EDITOR window above and below the data set.

HOW TO CREATE TEXT-BASED GRAPHICS

If, rather than loading a data set as you did previously, you had loaded a SAS program from a diskette in this way, you could simply execute it (run it) immediately. Now, however, you will learn how to write a SAS program that calls an external

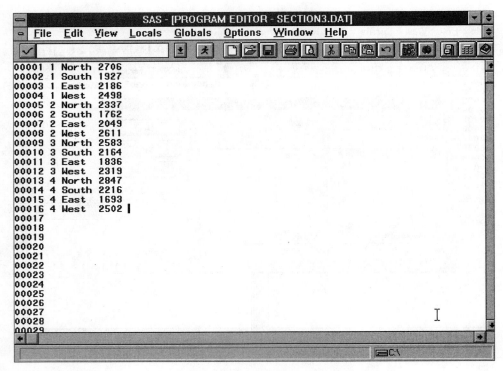

FIGURE 3.4   The Opened Datafile in the PROGRAM EDITOR Window

datafile. To do this, we need to write a separate SAS program that calls this datafile using an INFILE statement.

    Let us launch SAS for Windows again and then type in the first four lines of SAS code in the PROGRAM EDITOR window:

```
data graphics;
infile 'a:section3.dat';
input quarter region $ sales;
cards;
```

The DATA statement creates a SAS data set named graphics. The INFILE statement identifies the datafile we want the SAS program to read with an INPUT statement. The a:section3.dat means that the datafile section3.dat is stored on a diskette being inserted into the a: drive. The INPUT statement names three variables—quarter, region, and sales—where region is a qualitative variable as denoted by the $. Note that the INFILE statement must appear before the INPUT statement in the DATA step of a SAS program.

Now we will enter commands that, when executed, will call on SAS procedures that produce text-based graphical summaries of the data. First, we will call on the graphics capability of a procedure we have already seen in Assignment 2: PROC UNIVARIATE. Below the previous SAS code, type in

```
proc univariate plot;
var region sales;
run;
```

The plot option of the UNIVARIATE procedure produces a stem-and-leaf plot, a box plot, and a normal probability plot for quantitative variables. The alert reader may have noticed that by including the region variable, we are asking SAS for Windows to provide us with these plots for a qualitative (non-numerical) variable. This is an error, and we will see how to correct this error in the next section.

Below the entire UNIVARIATE procedure, we type in commands for a new SAS procedure, PROC CHART, which, when executed, will produce horizontal (HBAR statement) and vertical (VBAR statement) bar charts of the variable sales.

```
proc chart;
hbar sales;
vbar sales;
run;
```

The SAS program shown in Figure 3.5 should appear.

We should save this file now as a SAS program file. Click on File/Save as, and give your program a name with the .SAS extension. We named our program CHAPTER3.SAS. Remember to save the file to the diskette (a:), and not to the hard drive (c:), if the computer is not your own.

Now submit the program for execution by clicking on the running man icon in the toolbar.

HOW TO HANDLE PROGRAM ERRORS USING SAS LOG

You should always check your SAS log for errors or warnings. Click on Window/Log. Note that the SAS software has found an error (Figure 3.6).

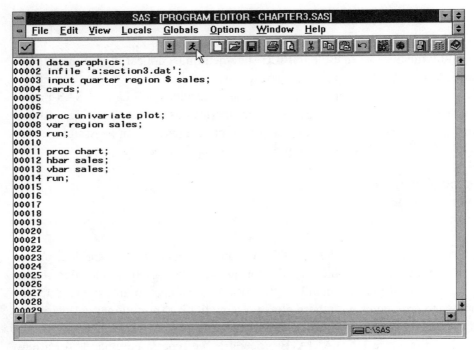

FIGURE 3.5 The Program for Producing Text-Based Charts

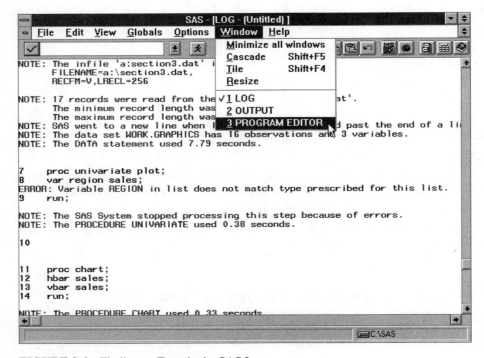

FIGURE 3.6 Finding an Error in the SAS Log

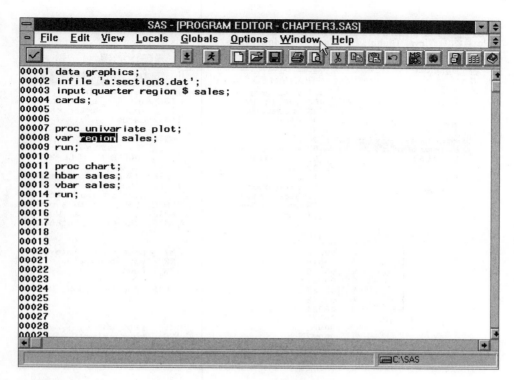

FIGURE 3.7   Correcting Our Error in the PROGRAM EDITOR

It's easy to spot the errors because they are printed in red:

ERROR: Variable REGION in list
does not match type prescribed for this list.

The computer is trying to tell you that the kind of graphs you asked for (box plots and the like) are applicable only to quantitative variables, not to qualitative variables like region. To correct this error, we need to go back to the PROGRAM EDITOR window. Click on Window/PROGRAM EDITOR.

If the PROGRAM EDITOR is blank, then click on Locals/Recall text. We want to remove the variable region from the VAR statement of PROC UNIVARIATE. One way to do this is to highlight the text by clicking and dragging so that the word region is in reverse (white on black) field and then hitting the *backspace* key on your keyboard (Figure 3.7).

You may want to clear the OUTPUT and LOG windows of the old materials. To do so, select each window in turn and click on Edit/Clear text (Figure 3.8).

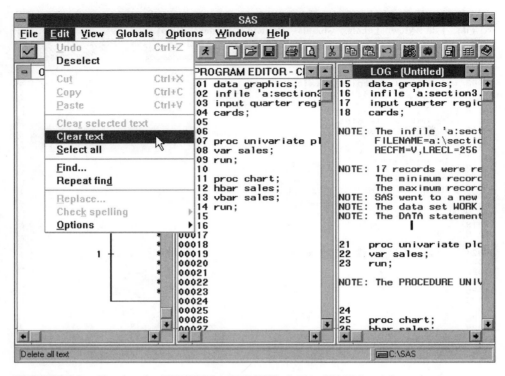

FIGURE 3.8   Clearing the OUTPUT and LOG Windows of Old Material

HOW TO PREVIEW YOUR OUTPUT BEFORE PRINTING

Once the error is fixed, save the program and submit it again. This time a check of the LOG window uncovers no errors or warnings, so we may proceed to examine the program results in the OUTPUT window.

Before we print out the results, we may want to preview the full printout pages to see how they will look when they are printed. Click on File/Print preview (Figure 3.9).

If you are preparing a report, you can then check out how your results will look page by page, zoom in for a closer look, or print out your results from within Print Preview (Figure 3.10).

HOW TO CREATE AND PRINT HIGH-RESOLUTION GRAPHICS

The SAS program can also produce beautiful high-resolution graphics. One way is to use PROC GCHART. Let's go back and alter the CHAPTER3.SAS program to produce these new graphics.

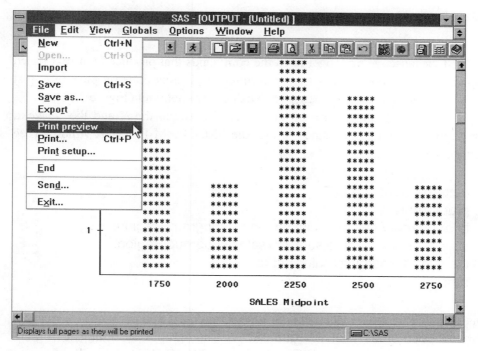

FIGURE 3.9   Getting Ready to Print Preview the Output

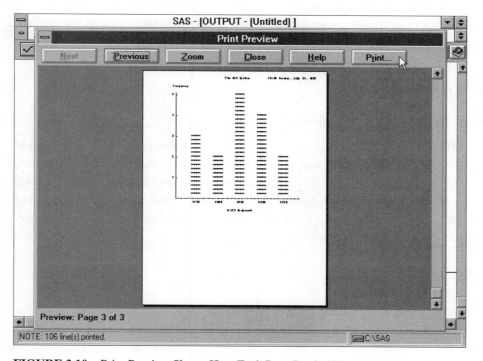

FIGURE 3.10   Print Preview Shows How Each Page Looks When Printed

First, because we no longer need the commands that produced our text-based graphics, we will *comment out* these commands. This is done by placing /* just above and */ just below the section you wish to comment out (Figure 3.11).

The SAS program ignores all code placed between the /* and the */. Next, type in the following commands in the The PROGRAM EDITOR window (see Figure 3.11):

```
pattern1 value=solid;
proc gchart;
hbar quarter / discrete sumvar=sales subgroup=region;
vbar quarter / discrete sumvar=sales subgroup=region;
pie quarter / sumvar=sales pct=outside;
run;
```

This use of PROC GCHART with the VBAR statement will produce a vertical bar chart of group sales totals by quarter, with sub-groups according to region. Specifying the HBAR or the PIE statements in PROC GCHART will produce a horizontal bar chart or a pie chart, respectively. Save the program and submit it. One of the resulting graphs, the vertical bar chart, is shown in Figure 3.12.

You can print the graph simply by clicking on the printer icon in the toolbar.

ON YOUR OWN

Hands-On Exercise 3: Graphical Methods

To learn how to use SAS graphical methods to summarize data, you should perform the following tasks step-by-step. Assume that there is a datafile named yourdata.dat on your own diskette, which has been inserted into the disk drive a:.

A test of *need for affiliation* has been given to 40 first-born and 50 later-born students. The results, put into three categories of need for affiliation—high, medium, and low—are shown here:

Later	High	10
Later	Medium	24
Later	Low	16
First	High	26
First	Medium	8
First	Low	6

```
File   Edit   View   Locals   Globals   Options   Window   Help
```

```
00001 data graphics;
00002 infile 'a:section3.dat';
00003 input quarter region $ sales;
00004 cards;
00005
00006 /*
00007 proc univariate plot;
00008 var sales;
00009 run;
00010
00011 proc chart;
00012 hbar sales;
00013 vbar sales;
00014 run;
00015 */
00016
00017 pattern1 value=solid;
00018 proc gchart;
00019 hbar quarter / discrete sumvar=sales subgroup=region;
00020 vbar quarter / discrete sumvar=sales subgroup=region;
00021 pie quarter / sumvar=sales pct=outside;
00022 run;
00023
00024
00025
00026
00027
00028
00029
```

C:\SAS

FIGURE 3.11   The Program for High-Resolution Graphics

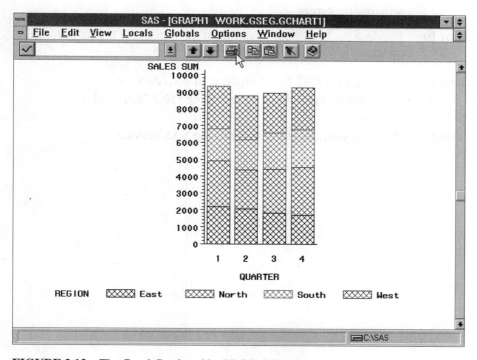

FIGURE 3.12   The Graph Produced by PROC GCHART

Using graphical methods with SAS for Windows, summarize the given data set.

Step 1:   Load the SAS software, and activate the PROGRAM EDITOR window.

Step 2:   Type in the DATA step of SAS code using the INFILE command.
➤   You can define the three input variables as *born*, *category*, and *result* where both *born* and *category* are non-numerical variables.

Step 3:   Type in the PROC step of SAS code for text-based graphics.

Step 4:   Run the SAS program, and check the LOG window for errors.

Step 5:   Preview the SAS output, and print the output.

Step 6:   Clear the OUTPUT and LOG windows of the old materials.

Step 7:   Recall the SAS program in the PROGRAM EDITOR window, and comment out the SAS code for text-based graphics.

Step 8:   Type in the new PROC step of SAS code for high-resolution graphics.

Step 9:   Again submit your SAS program to run, and check the LOG window for errors.

Step 10:   Preview the SAS output, and print the output for high-resolution graphics.

Step 11:   Save the new SAS program on your own diskette.
➤   You need to recall the program in the PROGRAM EDITOR window.

Step 12:   Print out your program, and exit the SAS session.

ASSIGNMENT 4

One-Sample t *Test*

OBJECTIVES

To perform a one-sample t test

To summarize the test results from the SAS output

One of the most commonly encountered problems in an introductory statistics course is that of testing a hypothesis regarding the value of a normal population mean μ when σ is unknown and the sample size is small ($n < 30$). This test is usually called a one-sample t test.

Let us start with this example. A therapist treating clients for communication apprehension (fear of public speaking) assessed the effectiveness of the treatment by giving her clients a standard test at the end of treatment. Here are the scores from 10 randomly selected clients:

$$65 \quad 58 \quad 55 \quad 75 \quad 81 \quad 89 \quad 74 \quad 70 \quad 63 \quad 72$$

Using an $\alpha = .05$ level of significance, test whether the mean test score of the therapist's clients after the treatment is higher than 65.

To test this hypothesis, we establish the following null and alternative hypotheses:

$$H_0: \mu \leq \mu_0$$
$$H_a: \mu > \mu_0$$

where $\mu_0 = 65$ denotes the specific numerical value being considered in the above hypotheses. In this assignment, you will learn how to perform a one-sample t test with SAS software and how to interpret the SAS output after running the program.

HOW TO WRITE A SAS PROGRAM
FOR THE ONE-SAMPLE *t* TEST

After launching SAS for Windows, we can type in a SAS example program in the PROGRAM EDITOR window (Figure 4.1).

```
─  SAS - [PROGRAM EDITOR - CHAPTER4.SAS]          ▼ ⬍
─  File  Edit  View  Locals  Globals  Options  Window  Help          ⬍
✓ │                      │ ± │ ⚡ │ □ 🖙 🖫 🖨 🖻 ✂ 🖹 🖺 ↶ 📇 ◉ 🗐 🖼 ◈
00001 data client;                                                    ✦
00002 title3 'One-Sample t Test';
00003 input scores @@;
00004 mu0=65;
00005 extra=scores-mu0;
00006 cards;
00007
00008 65 58 55 75 81 89 74 70 63 72
00009 ;
00010
00011 proc means n mean var std stderr maxdec=3;
00012 var scores;
00013 run;
00014
00015 proc means t prt;
00016 var extra;
00017 run;▮
00018
00019
00020
00021
00022
00023
00024
00025
00026
00027
00028
00029                                                                  ✦
← ▓▓▓▓▓▓▓▓▓▓▓▓▓▓▓▓▓▓▓▓▓▓▓▓▓▓▓▓▓▓▓▓▓▓▓▓▓▓▓▓▓▓▓▓▓▓▓▓▓▓▓▓▓▓▓▓▓▓ →
NOTE: 17 line(s) included.                          ▭C:\SAS
```

FIGURE 4.1   The Program for a One-Sample *t* Test

As you have learned, most SAS programs consist of two steps: the DATA step and the PROC step. In the DATA step of our example program, we first create a data set called client by using the following statement:

data client;

Our next SAS statement in the DATA step is the TITLE statement, which enables the program to print a title at the top of each page of output.

title3 'One-Sample t Test';

This statement means that the title One-Sample t Test will be printed on the third line of each page of output. The next statement is the INPUT statement:

input scores @@;

The variable is named scores. The @@ symbol (called a *double-trailing at-sign*) allows the program to read repeated sets of data values on one line. The next two lines of SAS code define the value of μ_0 (mu0) and the new variable extra:

```
mu0=65;
extra=scores–mu0;
```

The last statement in the DATA step is the **CARDS** statement:

```
cards;
```

The **CARDS** statement tells the computer that the data follow immediately.

As you can see in the data input portion of the program in Figure 4.1, several observations are entered on one line because the @@ symbol was used in the **INPUT** statement for the variable **scores**. The semicolon after the data set signals the end of the data.

In the PROC step of our example program, most of the sample statistics needed in making statistical inference on the mean μ can be obtained by calling on PROC MEANS along with the **VAR** statement to specify the names of the variables:

```
proc means n mean var std stderr maxdec=3;
var scores;
run;
```

The terms appearing after **means** in the PROC MEANS statement are called *options*. The options appearing in this MEANS procedure are **n**, **mean**, **var**, **std**, **stderr**, and **maxdec=3**. This portion of SAS code tells the program that the sample size, sample mean, variance, standard deviation, and standard error are to be computed for the variable **scores**, with the results printed out to at most three decimal places.

In the last portion of SAS code for the PROC step, the MEANS procedure is called again with the **t** and **prt** options, which ask for the observed value of the test statistic (**t**) and the *p*-value (**prt**) needed to test the null hypothesis $H_0\colon \mu \leq \mu_0$.

```
proc means t prt;
var extra;
run;
```

Notice that the variable used in this MEANS procedure is the new variable **extra**, which equals **scores–mu0**, as defined in the DATA step of the program. The reason for using the new variable **extra** here is that the **t** and **prt** options appearing in the MEANS procedure are needed for testing an equivalent null hypothesis $H_0\colon \mu - \mu_0 \leq 0$.

HOW TO INTERPRET THE SAS OUTPUT
FOR THE ONE-SAMPLE t TEST

Now we have finished typing in the SAS program for the one-sample t test. To run the program, we must submit it by clicking on the running man icon in the toolbar (see Figure 4.1).

Once we have submitted the SAS program, we should check the LOG window for errors. If there are no errors, we can look at the OUTPUT window. For example, in Figure 4.2, the OUTPUT window shows that the sample size n is 10, the sample mean $\bar{X}$ is 70.2, the sample variance S^2 is 107.733, the sample standard deviation S is 10.379, and the sample standard error $S/\sqrt{n}$ is 3.282. These statistics not only are needed for the hypothesis testing but also are used to construct confidence intervals for μ, σ^2, or σ. However, we do not discuss these confidence intervals in this handbook.

The OUTPUT window also provides the value of the test statistic T and its p-value for the one-sample t test. If you do not see these results in the OUTPUT window, then you should try scrolling down the window using the vertical scrollbar at the right. The results are shown in Figure 4.3. The observed value of the test statistic T, which is used to test the null hypothesis H_0: $\mu - \mu_0 \leq 0$, is 1.584. The p-value for this one-tailed test is 0.0738—that is, half of the printed value under Prob>|T|, or 0.1476/2. (If the observed value of the test statistic T is negative when the null hypothesis H_0: $\mu - \mu_0 \leq 0$, the p-value is $1 - $ Prob>|T|/2. For the null hypothesis H_0: $\mu - \mu_0 \geq 0$, the p-value is half of the printed value under Prob>|T| if the test statistic T is negative; the p-value is $1 - $ Prob>|T|/2 if the test statistic T is positive. If it is a two-tailed test, then the p-value is the printed value under Prob>|T|.)

Now let us use the p-value to draw the conclusion for our example. The rejection rule at a level of significance α applies:

If the p-value is less than α, the null hypothesis H_0 is rejected.

We already know that the p-value is 0.0738. With a level of significance of .05, we know that the p-value exceeds α; thus, the null hypothesis H_0: $\mu \leq \mu_0$ *cannot* be rejected. There is insufficient evidence to conclude that the mean test score of the therapist's clients after the treatment is higher than 65.

ON YOUR OWN

Hands-On Exercise 4: One-Sample t Test

You are now ready to test some hypotheses of your own using the one-sample t test. In order to practice the procedures you have learned in this assignment, you should perform the following tasks step-by-step.

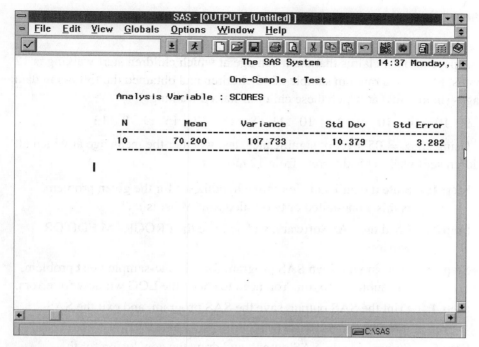

FIGURE 4.2   The Output from the One-Sample *t* Test

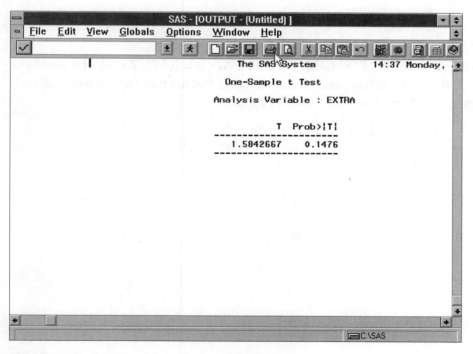

FIGURE 4.3   The Output from the One-Sample *t* Test

A psychologist claims that the mean age at which children start walking is 12 months. She took a random sample of 15 children and obtained the following data of ages (in months) at which these children started walking.

9   10   14   10   9   12   10   11   8   11   12   15   9   8   13

Using an $\alpha = .05$ level of significance, test whether the mean age at which all children start walking is different from 12 months.

Step 1: State the null and alternative hypotheses for the given problem. Is this a one-tailed or two-tailed test? What is μ_0?

Step 2: Load the SAS software, and activate the **PROGRAM EDITOR** window.

Step 3: Type in your own SAS program for this one-sample t test problem, and submit it to run. You need to check the **LOG** window for errors.

Step 4: Print the SAS output, save the SAS program, and exit the SAS session.

Step 5: Summarize the SAS output, and draw the conclusion for the problem.

> What is the p-value of the test?

Answer

$n = 15$, $\bar{X} = 10.733$, $S^2 = 4.495$, $S = 2.120$, $S/\sqrt{n} = 0.547$, $T = -2.314$, p-value = .0364. Reject the null hypothesis and conclude that the mean age at which all children start walking is different from 12 months.

ASSIGNMENT 5

Two-Sample t *Tests*

OBJECTIVES

To perform a two-independent-samples *t* test

To perform a two-matched-samples *t* test

The procedures that can be used to test hypotheses about the difference between the means of two normal populations for small-sample ($n_1 < 30$ and/or $n_2 < 30$) cases are called two-sample *t* tests. The samples can be classified into two types:

1. Two independent samples
2. Two matched samples

In this assignment, you will learn how to perform a *t* test for two independent samples and for two matched samples.

HOW TO PERFORM A *t* TEST FOR TWO INDEPENDENT SAMPLES

In the two-independent-samples case, the two samples are collected from two independent groups (populations), and the order of observations in each sample is not relevant.

Let us consider an example. A randomly assigned group of 13 participants learned a list of nonsense syllables while a tape of a speech by former President A was playing. A different group of 13 participants learned the same list of syllables while a tape of a speech by President B was playing. The number of presentations of the list before an errorless recital for each participant was as follows:

President A	26	13	10	24	24	25	23	20	16	13	15	19	22
President B	23	16	6	19	25	21	25	17	17	5	10	15	20

Using an $\alpha = .05$ level of significance, test to determine whether the two presidents' speeches made significant differences on the number of errorless presentations from each group.

To test whether there is a difference between the mean number of presentations of the list μ_1 from the group that heard former President A and the mean number of

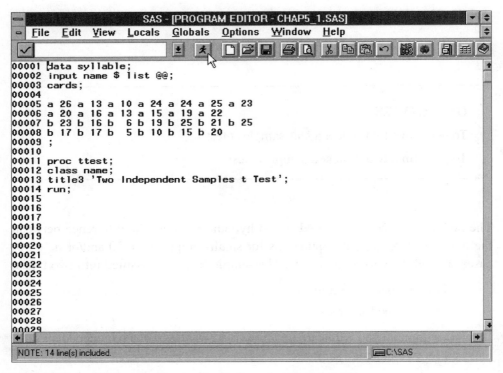

FIGURE 5.1   The Program for the Two-Independent-Samples *t* Test

presentations of the list μ_2 from the group that heard former President B, we establish the following null and alternative hypotheses:

$$H_0: \mu_1 = \mu_2$$
$$H_a: \mu_1 \neq \mu_2$$

Now we need to launch SAS for Windows and then type in a SAS example program in the PROGRAM EDITOR window (Figure 5.1).

Let us examine the SAS code used for this problem. First, we create a data set named **syllable** and define two variables called **name** and **list**. The $ symbol indicates that the variable **name** is not numeric. The @@ symbol means that there will be more than one observation entered per line in the data set after the CARDS statement.

```
data syllable;
input name $ list @@;
cards;
```

The variable name has two qualitative values—a (President A) and b (President B) in the data set representing the two groups being compared. Again, as you have learned, the semicolon after the data set signals the end of the data.

The two-independent-samples *t* test is performed by calling on PROC TTEST with the CLASS statement. The CLASS statement provides the name of the grouping variable, which in the two-independent-samples *t* test case must have only two values.

```
proc ttest;
class name;
title3 'Two Independent Samples t Test';
run;
```

The title3 statement tells the SAS program that the title Two Independent Samples t Test will be printed on the third line of output.

Now let us see how to interpret the SAS output for the two-independent-samples *t* test. Of course, we have to submit the SAS program first and then check the LOG window for errors. If there are no errors, then the *t* test results are displayed in the OUTPUT window (Figure 5.2). You need to scroll the window to the right using the horizontal scrollbar at the bottom to obtain a complete look at the SAS output.

For each of the two groups, the output displays the sample size, sample mean, sample standard deviation, and sample standard error. PROC TTEST computes the *t* statistic and its corresponding degrees of freedom based on the assumption that the population variances of the two groups are equal. If the population variances are unequal, PROC TTEST computes an approximate *t* statistic and its corresponding degrees of freedom using Satterthwaite's method. In addition, an F statistic is computed to test for equality of the two population variances.

The value of the F statistic used to compare variances is 1.51. The *p*-value for the two-tailed F test is 0.4843. Because this value exceeds .05, we conclude that $\sigma_1^2 = \sigma_2^2$ and use the equal variances procedure to compare means. The observed value of the test statistic T is 1.0216, and it is used to test the null hypothesis $H_0: \mu_1 = \mu_2$. The *p*-value for this two-tailed test is 0.3172. (For the null hypothesis $H_0: \mu_1 \geq \mu_2$, the *p*-value is half of the printed value under Prob>|T| if the test statistic T is negative; the *p*-value is 1−Prob>|T|/2 if the test statistic T is positive. For the null hypothesis $H_0: \mu_1 \leq \mu_2$, the *p*-value is half of the printed value under Prob>|T| if the test statistic T is positive; the *p*-value is 1−Prob>|T|/2 if the test statistic T is negative.) This *p*-value of 0.3172 is larger than our level of significance of $\alpha = .05$; thus, the null hypothesis $H_0: \mu_1 = \mu_2$ *cannot* be rejected.

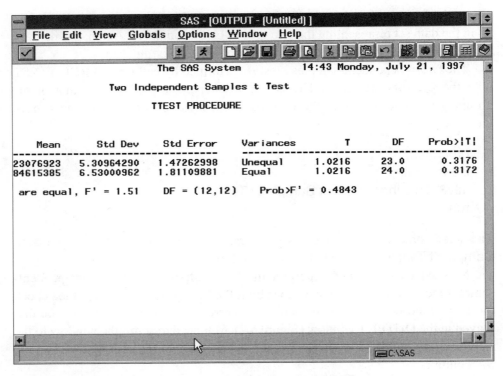

FIGURE 5.2   The Output from the Two-Independent-Samples *t* Test

We conclude that the two presidents' speeches had no significant differences on the number of errorless presentations from each group.

Notice that if the *p*-value (Prob>F) for the two-tailed *F* test is small (say, less than .05), then we conclude that $\sigma_1^2 \neq \sigma_2^2$ and have to use the unequal variances procedure to compare means.

HOW TO RUN A *t* TEST FOR TWO MATCHED SAMPLES

In the two-matched-samples test, each observation in one sample is paired with an observation in the other. This sampling procedure often leads to a smaller sampling error than in the two-independent-samples procedure.

Let's consider the following example. A study is performed to determine how alcohol affects the brain's response to sound. The researchers measure brain responses in six participants both before and after the subjects drink an alcoholic beverage. The results are as follows:

Person	1	2	3	4	5	6
Before	5.80	5.88	5.38	5.40	5.90	5.71
After	5.90	6.05	5.64	5.58	6.05	5.87

Using $\alpha = .05$, test to determine whether alcohol ingestion affects brain response to sound.

To develop a test for the two matched samples, we must take into account the fact that each matched pair of observations is produced by the same person. Therefore, we can define a new random variable d as the difference between brain responses for each person after and before the subject drinks an alcoholic beverage, or d = after – before. Now the original two-matched-samples problem can be reduced to a one-sample problem for the variable d. Thus, testing whether alcohol ingestion affects brain response to sound is equivalent to testing the following null and alternative hypotheses:

$$H_0: \mu_d = 0$$
$$H_a: \mu_d \neq 0$$

where μ_d is the mean of the population of differences d.

Let us launch SAS for Windows again and then type in a new SAS example program in the PROGRAM EDITOR window (Figure 5.3). In the DATA step of the example program, we create a data set called brain and define three variables—person, before, and after—by using the INPUT statement. Then we create the new variable d that equals after–before. The data set is entered right after the CARDS statement.

```
data brain;
input person before after;
d=after–before;
cards;
```

In the PROC step of the example program, PROC MEANS is called on to test $H_0: \mu_d = 0$, and the mean, variance, standard deviation, and standard error are computed for the variable d, with the results printed out to at most three decimal places.

```
proc means mean var std stderr t prt maxdec=3;
var d;
title3 'Two Matched Samples t Test';
run;
```

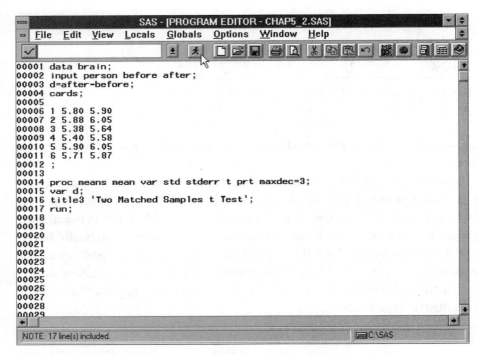

FIGURE 5.3 The Program for the Two-Matched-Samples *t* Test

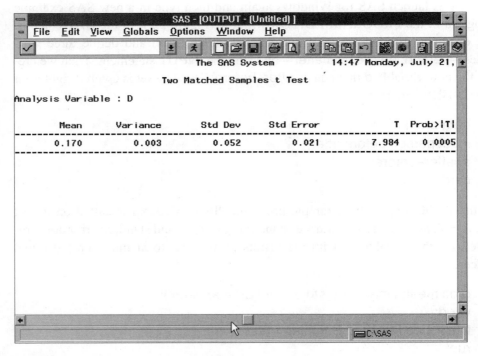

FIGURE 5.4 The Output from the Two-Matched-Samples *t* Test

The value of the test statistic T and its p-value are also reported. The title Two Matched Samples t Test is printed on the third line of the SAS output.

Once we submit the SAS program, we are ready to interpret the SAS output (Figure 5.4) for the two-matched-samples t test. As we saw in Assignment 4, the OUTPUT window shows that the sample mean $\bar{d}$ is 0.170, the sample variance S_d^2 is 0.003, the sample standard deviation S_d is 0.052, and the sample standard error $S_d/\sqrt{n}$ is 0.021. In addition, the observed value of the T statistic that is used to test the null hypothesis $H_0: \mu_d = 0$ is $T = 7.984$. The p-value for this two-tailed test is 0.0005. Using $\alpha = .05$, we see that the p-value is less than α; thus, the null hypothesis $H_0: \mu_d = 0$ is rejected. We conclude that alcohol ingestion significantly affects brain response to sound.

ON YOUR OWN

Hands-On Exercise 5.1: Two-Independent-Samples t _Test_

To better learn how to run the two-independent-samples t test, you should perform the following tasks step-by-step.

A social psychologist was interested in how communication patterns can affect creative problem solving in small groups. Seven groups of each of two types were formed: vertical and horizontal. In the vertical groups, participants were organized hierarchically, so that they could communicate and share information only with the people above or below them. In the horizontal groups, there was no hierarchy; participants could communicate with all other group members. All groups worked on a series of complex problems, and the number of solutions produced by each group is shown here:

Vertical group	13	12	11	11	9	8	8
Horizontal group	13	15	12	15	18	10	14

Using the 5% level of significance, test whether the groups had any significant difference on the number of solutions produced.

Step 1: State the null and alternative hypotheses for the given problem.
➤ Is this a one-tailed or two-tailed test?

Step 2: Load the SAS software, and activate the PROGRAM EDITOR window.

Step 3: Type in your own SAS program for this two-independent-samples t test problem, and submit the SAS program to run. You need to check out the LOG window for errors.

Step 4:   Print the SAS output, save the SAS program, and exit the SAS session.

Step 5:   Summarize the SAS output, and draw the conclusion for the problem. What is the *p*-value of the test?

Answer

The test statistic $T = 2.9327$; this T value could be -2.9327 depending on which group is called μ_1 and which is called μ_2. The degrees of freedom of the T value are 12, and the *p*-value is .0125. Reject the null hypothesis and conclude that the groups had significant differences on the number of solutions produced.

Hands-On Exercise 5.2: Two-Matched-Samples t Test

To better understand how to run the two-matched-samples *t* test, you should perform the following tasks step-by-step.

Suppose we are interested in the effect of muscle relaxation on anxiety. We select seven people and test their anxiety using a standard scale. The participants then receive five sessions of relaxation training, and their anxiety level is once again tested. The data are given here.

Person	1	2	3	4	5	6	7
Before	9	2	12	17	8	5	10
After	6	1	8	11	3	6	7

Using $\alpha = .05$, test whether the relaxation training significantly reduced anxiety.

Step 1:   State the null and alternative hypotheses for the given problem.
➤   Is this a one-tailed or two-tailed test?

Step 2:   Load the SAS software, and activate the PROGRAM EDITOR window.

Step 3:   Type in your own SAS program for this two-matched-samples *t* test problem, defining the new variable *d*. Then submit the SAS program to run. You need to check out the LOG window for errors.

Step 4:   Print the SAS output, save the SAS program, and exit the SAS session.

Step 5: Summarize the SAS output, and draw the conclusion for the problem. What is the *p*-value of the test?

Answer

d = after – before, $\bar{d}$ = –3.0, S_d^2 = 5.667, S_d = 2.380, $S_d/\sqrt{n}$ = 0.900, T = –3.334, *p*-value = .0079. Reject the null hypothesis and conclude that the relaxation training significantly reduced anxiety.

ASSIGNMENT 6

One-Way ANOVA

OBJECTIVES

To perform one-way ANOVA

To interpret the results from the SAS output

HOW TO PERFORM ANOVA

In Assignment 5, we learned how to compare the population means from two populations or treatment groups. However, researchers often need to compare means from more than two groups.

For example, a quality control specialist might be interested in whether there were significant differences in mean customer satisfaction levels at his company's four retail outlets. Performing *t* tests for each pair of stores would be time-consuming; it might miss the overall picture; and it could, in fact, lead to questionable conclusions concerning simultaneous inference (more on this later).

The preferred analytical method is to perform *analysis of variance* (ANOVA), which compares population means across several groups.

Suppose you are an investigator researching the development of object permanence in young children. Object permanence is the recognition that an object continues to exist even if the child cannot see it. You have collected data on the presence of this trait in three groups of 10 children, ages 9 months, 12 months, and 15 months. The data consist of scores of how many times (out of 10) the child manifested object permanence in an experiment. Suppose you would like to determine whether there are differences among the three groups. The way to do this is to conduct an analysis of variance.

One way to perform ANOVA with SAS software is to use PROC ANOVA. This procedure is appropriate when you have balanced data, meaning there are the same number of sample observations from each group. If your data are unbalanced you should use PROC GLM instead. The basic syntax of PROC ANOVA is:

```
PROC anova;
CLASS variable;
MODEL dependent variable = effects;
```

PROC ANOVA calls on the SAS procedure to perform the analysis of variance. The **CLASS** statement specifies the names of the variables by which the groups are classified. This assignment has only one class variable; Assignment 7 will have two class variables. Your class variables may be numeric or character, but they should always be categorical. The **CLASS** statement must appear in your ANOVA procedure before the **MODEL** statement. The **MODEL** statement specifies which variables are dependent and which are independent effects. The dependent variable is the response variable whose mean you are comparing across populations. In this assignment, we have only one effect (sometimes called *treatment*), which implies that we are performing *one-way ANOVA*. In Assignment 7, we will consider how to compare population means with respect to two effects; that is, we will perform *two-way ANOVA*.

AN EXAMPLE USING PROC ANOVA

Let's do an example. Type in the following lines in the PROGRAM EDITOR window, and submit it, as in Figure 6.1:

```
data object;
input agegroup score @@;
cards;

1 8 1 3 1 4 1 6 1 5 1 4 1 9 1 2 1 0 1 1
2 10 2 5 2 6 2 7 2 6 2 5 2 10 2 3 2 3 2 3
3 10 3 8 3 9 3 9 3 8 3 7 3 9 3 6 3 6 3 8
;

proc anova;
class agegroup;
model score = agegroup;
run;
```

As usual, the DATA step names the data set, **object**, and two variables, **agegroup** and **score**, and inputs the data after the **CARDS** statement. The first statement in the PROC step is

```
proc anova;
```

which tells the computer that you would like to perform ANOVA. The data set of interest is the last defined data set, **object**. The second line of the PROC step is

```
class agegroup;
```

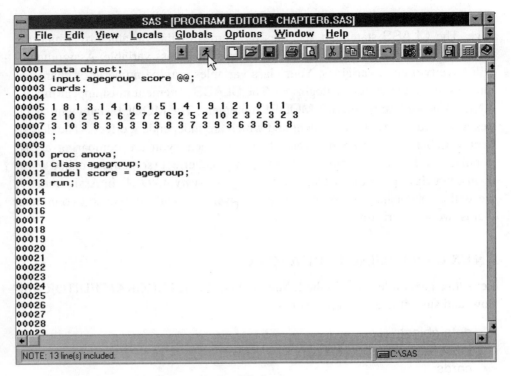

FIGURE 6.1   The Program for Analysis of Variance

which specifies that our class variable is **agegroup**, representing the three developmental age groups in the experiment (9 months, 12 months, and 15 months). At this point in the program, we know that we will be comparing population means of some response variable across these three age group categories. The third line in the PROC step is

    model score = agegroup;

which indicates that the object permanence score recorded by the investigator (**score**) is our response variable and that we wish to compare the score means across the different age group categories. Finally, don't forget the last line of the PROC step,

    run;

which tells the computer to execute the ANOVA procedure.

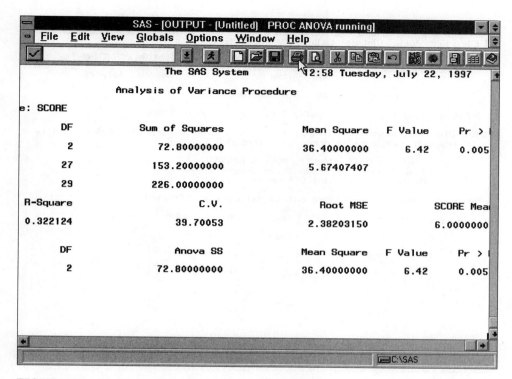

FIGURE 6.2   The Output from the Analysis of Variance

When the program is typed in, submit it and check SAS log for errors (click on Window/LOG). If there are no errors, take a look at the output (click on Window/OUTPUT).

INTERPRETING THE OUTPUT

The first page of the ANOVA output gives the class level information, stating which variable is your class variable, what your various subcategories are, and how many observations you have in your data set.

The second page of the ANOVA output contains the core of your results (Figure 6.2). The ANOVA table presents a great deal of information: source of variation, degrees of freedom, sum of squares, and mean squares for the *Model* (also called *between*) term and the *Error* (*within*) term, as well as the F statistic and its *p*-value.

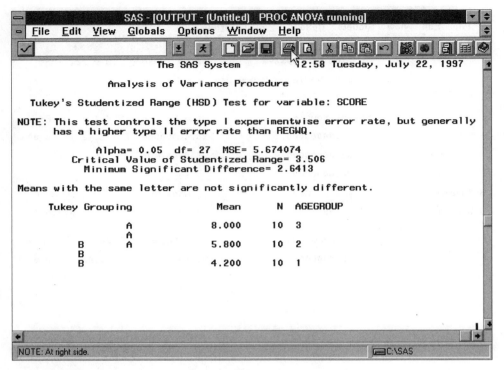

FIGURE 6.3   The Output from the Pairwise Comparison

The null hypothesis for analysis of variance is that the population means of the response variable are equal across all levels of the class variable. Perhaps the most important single number in your ANOVA output is the *p*-value, shown as Pr > F. When the *p*-value is small (for example, less than your chosen level of significance), this casts doubt on the null hypothesis. The *p*-value for this ANOVA is fairly small (0.0053), providing good evidence that the null hypothesis should be rejected. In other words, there is evidence that not all true object permanence score means are equal across the various developmental age groups.

We may wish to perform pairwise comparisons to determine which groups indeed differ and which do not. A series of *t* tests would run into problems concerning simultaneous inference (the achieved level of significance would not equal the stated level). Therefore, special statistical procedures have been developed to perform these post-hoc simultaneous pairwise comparisons. To do this in SAS for Windows, simply add the following line after your **MODEL** statement:

```
means agegroup / scheffe tukey bon;
```

This calls upon the **MEANS** statement of PROC ANOVA—specifically, the **Scheffe, Tukey,** and **Bonferroni** options for simultaneous pairwise comparisons. Make sure you specify your class variable (here it is **agegroup**).

Figure 6.3 shows part of the ouput for Tukey's studentized range test. Look at the letters under the phrase **Tukey Grouping**. The letter **A** is repeated for age groups **2** and **3** (12 and 15 months); the letter **B** is repeated for age groups **1** and **2** (9 and 12 months). This indicates that the means for these pairs do not differ significantly from each other. However, you will notice that groups **1** and **3** do not share the same letter. This indicates that their means differ significantly. All of these results are valid simultaneously with an overall significance level of $\alpha = .05$, as indicated on this page of the output.

Sometimes, SAS presents its pairwise comparison results somewhat differently. In this case, each pairwise combination is listed, and the pairs that differ significantly are marked with ***.

ON YOUR OWN

Hands-On Exercise 6: Analysis of Variance

To better understand how to use the analysis of variance, you should perform the following tasks step-by-step.

Suppose you are investigating whether the presence of others inhibits a subject's ability to perform complex tasks quickly and correctly. Response latency times were recorded for tasks performed alone (1-person group), in the presence of another person (2-person group), or in the presence of three other persons (4-person group). Use analysis of variance to determine whether group differences exist in the mean time to complete the tasks. If you find significant differences, do a pairwise comparison to determine which pairs differ. Here are the data; note that the four-person group has one missing observation.

1PG	0.55	1.23	0.25	0.36	1.16	0.15	0.80
2PG	1.55	2.69	1.10	0.85	0.75	1.25	3.16
4PG	3.28	2.15	5.63	1.18	4.75	2.65	miss

Step 1: Peruse the data set. Do there appear to be differences between the groups? This should give you a preliminary idea of whether you will find significance in the ANOVA.

Step 2: Load the SAS software and activate the PROGRAM EDITOR window.

Step 3: Type in your own SAS program to generate the analysis of variance, along with the pairwise comparisons analysis. Submit your program, and check the LOG window for errors.

Step 4: Print the SAS output, save your SAS program, and exit the SAS session.

Step 5: Interpret your SAS output.
➤ Examine the ANOVA output. Is the *p*-value (Pr > F) small enough to indicate that significant differences exist among the groups?
➤ Examine the pairwise comparison results. Which pairs of groups are significantly different. Do you find this surprising?

Answer

Perusal of the data set seems to indicate that differences may exist in the true group means. For example, almost all times for the 1-person group are faster than almost all times for the 3-person group. Consider the ANOVA output. The *p*-value of .0017 is much smaller than the usual levels of significance such as .01 or .05. This is evidence that there are differences among the groups in true mean response times. Which group pairs are significantly different? Examine the pairwise comparison output. These results indicate that the 1-person group mean differs significantly from the 4-person group mean, but not the 2-person group mean. The 2-person and 4-person group means also differ significantly. This is not particularly surprising, as many complex tasks require concentration levels not amenable to groups.

ASSIGNMENT 7

Two-Way ANOVA

OBJECTIVES

To perform a randomized block design

To perform a two-factor factorial design

In Assignment 6, we studied how to test for the equality of population means from several groups. The statistical procedure used there is called one-way ANOVA (analysis of variance), in which only one factor is of concern. In this assignment, we consider two different experimental designs involving more than one factor of interest. The procedure used here is called two-way ANOVA, and the two experimental designs are:

1. A randomized block design
2. A two-factor factorial design

In this assignment, you will learn first how to perform a randomized block design and then how to run a two-factor factorial design using SAS software.

HOW TO PERFORM A RANDOMIZED BLOCK DESIGN

The randomized block design is used to compare the means of several populations in the presence of an extraneous factor. The extraneous factor is considered the block factor and is used to control some of the extraneous sources of variation, as well as to reduce the experimental error variability.

To illustrate, let us consider the following example. In a study of the effect of fatigue on performance of simple tasks, five volunteers were instructed to perform a data entry task as rapidly and as accurately as possible. Because of potential differences among the volunteers, the volunteers were used as randomized blocks in the experiment. The number of errors committed by each volunteer during four 15-minute time periods was recorded:

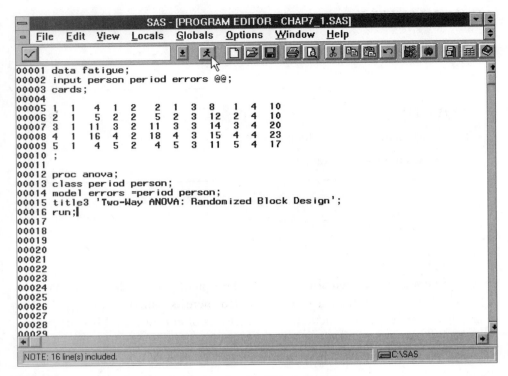

FIGURE 7.1   The Program for the Randomized Block Design

Person	1st 15 Min.	2nd 15 Min.	3rd 15 Min.	4th 15 Min.
1	4	2	8	10
2	5	5	12	10
3	11	11	14	20
4	16	18	15	23
5	4	4	11	17

Using $\alpha = .05$, we can test to see whether fatigue influenced performance.

The four time periods are the factor of interest and are called *treatments*. The five volunteers were utilized as an extraneous factor to reduce the variation of the experimental error and are called *blocks*. We are interested in testing the equality of the treatment means, or the following null hypothesis:

H_0: All treatment means are equal (that is, fatigue did not affect performance)

Let us launch SAS for Windows and then type in a SAS example program in the PROGRAM EDITOR window (Figure 7.1). In the DATA step, we create a data set named fatigue and define three variables—person, period, and errors—by using the INPUT statement. The period is coded as 1 (first 15 minutes), 2 (second 15 minutes), 3 (third 15 minutes), and 4 (fourth 15 minutes), while the person is categorized by 1, 2, 3, 4, and 5. The @@ symbol means that there will be more than one observation for each variable entered per line in the data set after the CARDS statement, and the semicolon after the data set signals the end of the data.

```
data fatigue;
input person period errors @@;
cards;
1  1   4  1  2   2  1  3   8  1  4  10
2  1   5  2  2   5  2  3  12  2  4  10
3  1  11  3  2  11  3  3  14  3  4  20
4  1  16  4  2  18  4  3  15  4  4  23
5  1   4  5  2   4  5  3  11  5  4  17
;
```

In the PROC step of the program, the ANOVA test is performed by calling on PROC ANOVA with the CLASS and the MODEL statements. The CLASS statement must appear before the MODEL statement in the ANOVA procedure. For the two-way ANOVA, the CLASS statement provides two grouping variables, such as the period and person variables in our example. In the randomized block design, the MODEL statement is always stated in this form:

model *dependent variable = treatments blocks;*

In this example, errors is the dependent variable, period is the treatments (the factor of interest), and person is the blocks (the extraneous factor). The title3 statement tells the computer to print the title Two-Way ANOVA: Randomized Block Design on the third line of output.

```
proc anova;
class period person;
model errors = period person;
title3 'Two-Way ANOVA: Randomized Block Design';
run;
```

When you have finished typing in the entire SAS program, you need to submit the program and then check the LOG window for errors. If there are no errors, then the results of the randomized block design are displayed in the OUTPUT window

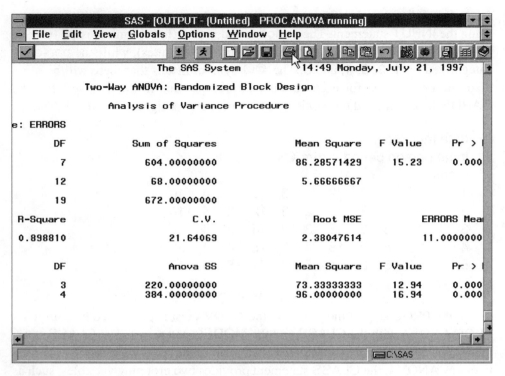

FIGURE 7.2   The Output from the Randomized Block Design

(Figure 7.2). You need to scroll down the window using the vertical scrollbar at the right to get a complete look at the SAS output.

The results obtained can be summarized in the following ANOVA table.

Source of Variation	Degrees of Freedom	Sum of Squares	Mean Square	F Value	p-Value
Treatments	3	220	73.33	12.94	0.0005
Blocks	4	384	96		
Error	12	68	5.67		
Total	19	672			

It is important to see how to interpret the results of the randomized block design. Here, the F value used to test differences between treatment means is **12.94**, with **3** numerator degrees of freedom and **12** denominator degrees of freedom. The p-value for testing the null hypothesis of the equality of the treatment means is 0.0005. This p-value is less than our α of .05; thus, the null hypothesis H_0 is rejected. We conclude that fatigue significantly affected performance.

Notice that the ANOVA table does not provide an F value for the blocks (the variable person). This is because the experiment was designed to test the factor of four 15-minute time periods, not the factor of the volunteers. Using the F value for the blocks to test for significance of the blocks is improper. However, to make an evaluation about whether the block factor in the experiment is necessary, we can get the F value for the blocks from the SAS output. If the F value is considerably larger than 1, then the block factor in the experiment is helpful in improving the precision of the comparison of treatment means. If the F value is much less than 1, then the block factor is not necessary in the experiment and a complete random-ized design (one-way ANOVA) should be preferred in future experiments. There are no clear answers where the F value for the blocks is near to 1.

In our example, we can see in Figure 7.2 that the F value for the blocks (the variable person) is 16.94. Because this value exceeds 1, we believe that using those five volunteers as the blocks in the experiment is beneficial.

HOW TO RUN A TWO-FACTOR FACTORIAL DESIGN

Now we are concerned with investigations of the simultaneous effects of two fac-tors, where neither factor is considered extraneous and both are of equal concern. This experiment is called a *two-factor factorial design*. The term *factorial* is used because all possible combinations of factor levels for the different factors are included in the experiment. One advantage of the two-factor factorial design is that we can test for the presence of an *interaction* between the two factors.

To illustrate, consider the next example. A two-factor factorial experiment with four replicates has been done to test the effects of expressed aggression in the home and dose level of an antipsychotic drug on schizophrenic behavior. Factor A is the level of expressed aggression (low, medium, high), and factor B is the drug dose (low, high). The dependent variable is the number of schizophrenic symp-toms in a 4-hour observation session. The results are shown in the following table.

	Factor B							
Factor A	Low				High			
Low	16	20	10	15	8	10	14	12
Medium	20	20	15	15	12	10	10	11
High	25	26	28	30	17	12	12	15

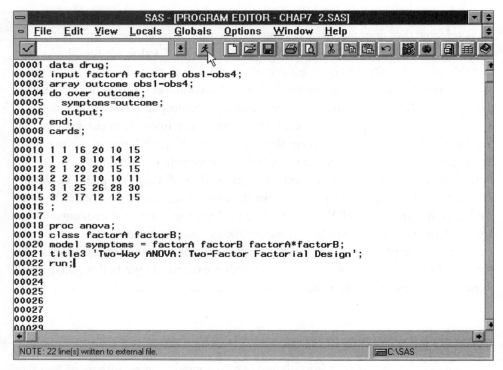

FIGURE 7.3   The Program for the Two-Factor Factorial Design

Using $\alpha = .05$, test for any significant effects from factor A, factor B, or an interaction between the two factors.

In this example, we are interested in testing the following three null hypotheses:

1. H_0: There are no effects from factor A.

2. H_0: There are no effects from factor B.

3. H_0: There are no effects from the interaction between factor A and factor B.

Now let us launch SAS for Windows and type in a SAS example program in the PROGRAM EDITOR window (Figure 7.3). In the DATA step of the program, we create a data set called drug and define six variables—factorA, factorB, and obs1-obs4—by using the INPUT statement. Notice that obs1-obs4 is not obs1 *minus* obs4. FactorA is classified as 1 (low), 2 (medium), and 3 (high), and factorB by 1 (low) and 2 (high). The four variables obs1, obs2, obs3, and obs4 represent the observations of the experiment at each combination of factor levels.

```
data drug;
input factorA factorB obs1-obs4;
```

The next five lines of SAS code combine four replicates in each cell to be read by the computer without our having to repeat factor level codes. The new variable outcome is established by using the ARRAY statement to represent the list of variables obs1-obs4. The DO OVER statement automatically executes the commands between the DO OVER and the END statements for each element of the outcome. The variable symptoms contains the four replicates at each combination of factor levels. The OUTPUT statement tells the computer to output the current observation to the data set drug. The data are entered right after the CARDS statement, and the semicolon after the data set signals the end of the data.

```
array outcome obs1-obs4;
do over outcome;
    symptoms = outcome;
    output;
end;
cards;

1   1   16   20   10   15
1   2    8   10   14   12
2   1   20   20   15   15
2   2   12   10   10   11
3   1   25   26   28   30
3   2   17   12   12   15
;
```

In the PROC step of the program, as we learned in Assignment 6, the ANOVA test is accomplished by calling on PROC ANOVA with the CLASS and MODEL statements. Again, the CLASS statement must appear before the MODEL statement. For the two-way ANOVA, the CLASS statement specifies two grouping variables. In this example, the two grouping variables are factorA and factorB. In the two-factor factorial design, the MODEL statement follows this general form:

model *dependent variable = factorA factorB factorA*factorB;*

In this example, symptoms is the dependent variable. The title3 statement tells the computer to print the title Two-Way ANOVA: Two-Factor Factorial Design at the third line of output.

proc anova;

```
┌──────────────────────────────────────────────────────────────────────────┐
│  ─      SAS - [OUTPUT - [Untitled]   PROC ANOVA running]         ▼  ┆      │
│  ─   File   Edit   View   Globals   Options   Window   Help           ┆    │
│  ┌─✓──────────────────┐  ┌─┐ ┌─┐ □ ▭ ▣ ▤ ▥ ▦ ▧ ↺ ▨ ● ▤ ▦ ◈         │
│                    The SAS System            14:54 Monday, July 21, 1997 ▲│
│              Two-Way ANOVA: Two-Factor Factorial Design                   │
│                     Analysis of Variance Procedure                        │
│ e: SYMPTOMS                                                               │
│      DF            Sum of Squares        Mean Square    F Value    Pr > │
│       5            743.70833333          148.74166667     20.40    0.000 │
│      18            131.25000000            7.29166667                     │
│      23            874.95833333                                          │
│   R-Square             C.V.               Root MSE        SYMPTOMS Mea   │
│   0.849993           16.92099            2.70030862         15.9583333   │
│       DF             Anova SS            Mean Square    F Value    Pr > │
│        2            265.33333333         132.66666667     18.19    0.000 │
│        1            392.04166667         392.04166667     53.77    0.000 │
│        2             86.33333333          43.16666667      5.92    0.010 │
│                                                                          ▼│
│  ◄├───────────────────────────────────────────────────────────────┤►    │
│                                                    ▷   ▭C:\SAS           │
└──────────────────────────────────────────────────────────────────────────┘
```

FIGURE 7.4   The Output from the Two-Factor Factorial Design

class factorA factorB;
model symptoms = factorA factorB factorA*factorB;
title3 'Two-Way ANOVA: Two-Factor Factorial Design';
run;

Once you have finished typing in the SAS program, submit the program, and then check the LOG window for errors. If there are no errors, the results of the two-factor factorial design are displayed in the OUTPUT window (Figure 7.4). You also need to scroll the window to the right using the horizontal scrollbar at the bottom of the screen to obtain a complete look at the SAS output.

The results of the two-factor factorial design from the SAS output (see Figure 7.4) are summarized in the following ANOVA table:

Source of Variation	Degrees of Freedom	Sum of Squares	Mean Square	F Value	p-Value
Factor A	2	265.33	132.67	18.19	0.0001
Factor B	1	392.04	392.04	53.77	0.0001
Interaction	2	86.33	43.17	5.92	0.0106
Error	18	131.25	7.29		
Total	23	874.95			

Now let us draw conclusions about any significant effects due to Factor A, Factor B, and the interaction from the above ANOVA table. We are interested in testing the three given null hypotheses.

For Factor A, the F value is given as 18.19, with 2 numerator degrees of freedom and 18 denominator degrees of freedom. The p-value associated with the F value is 0.0001, which is less than $\alpha = .05$. We reject null hypothesis 1 of no effects from Factor A.

For Factor B, the F value is shown as 53.77, with 1 numerator degree of freedom and 18 denominator degrees of freedom. The p-value of this F value is 0.0001, which is also less than $\alpha = .05$. We reject null hypothesis 2 of no effects from Factor B.

For the interaction between the two factors, the F value is given as 5.92, with 2 numerator degrees of freedom and 18 denominator degrees of freedom. The p-value of the F value is 0.0106, which again is less than $\alpha = .05$. We reject null hypothesis 3 of no interaction between the two factors.

Therefore, we conclude that the number of schizophrenic symptoms is significantly affected by the interaction between the level of expressed aggression and the drug dose. Furthermore, the main effects are significant: Both the level of expressed aggression and the drug dose appear to have a significant effect on the number of schizophrenic symptoms.

ON YOUR OWN

Hands-On Exercise 7.1: Randomized Block Design

To better understand how to run the randomized block design, you should perform the following tasks step-by-step.

Six student volunteers were deprived of sleep for varying periods, and their performance on a pursuit rotor task was measured. The object of the pursuit rotor task is to keep a stylus in contact with a spot on a rotating turntable. It is primarily a measure of hand-eye coordination and should be sensitive to the effects of sleep deprivation. Because of potential differences among volunteers, the randomized block design was conducted and the six volunteers were used as blocks in the experiment. The length of the deprivation and the amount of time during a 1-minute test that each student could keep the stylus in contact with the target are shown in the following table. Using $\alpha = .05$, determine whether lack of sleep affected performance on the task. People scoring 0 often fell asleep at the start of a session.

Sleep Deprivation

Student	0 Hr.	24 Hr.	48 Hr.	72 Hr.
1	30	10	5	5
2	45	10	10	3
3	15	5	5	5
4	20	15	5	0
5	30	20	0	0
6	35	10	20	6

Step 1: State the null and alternative hypotheses for the problem.

Step 2: Load the SAS software, and activate the PROGRAM EDITOR window.

Step 3: Type in your own SAS program for this randomized block design, and submit the program to run. You need to check the LOG window for errors.

Step 4: Print the SAS output, save the SAS program, and exit the SAS session.

Step 5: Summarize the results from the SAS output in an ANOVA table. Interpret the results.

➤   Examine whether the block factor is necessary in this experiment.

Answer

The F value for treatments is 17.63, with 3 numerator degrees of freedom and 15 denominator degrees of freedom. Its p-value is .0001, which is less than α. Hence, lack of sleep significantly affected performance on the task. The F value for the blocks is 1.41, which is close to 1. This indicates that using those six student volunteers as the blocks in the experiment may or may not be useful.

Hands-On Exercise 7.2: Two-Factor Factorial Design

To better learn how to run the two-factor factorial design, you should perform the following tasks step-by-step.

The data shown in the following table are for a two-factor factorial design with three replicates.

	Factor B								
Factor A	1			2			3		
1	2,	6,	6	6,	4,	9	1,	3,	6
2	4,	5,	3	2,	4,	2	9,	11,	8
3	7,	8,	10	1,	0,	3	3,	7,	6
4	9,	10,	6	10,	12,	9	6,	7,	5

Using $\alpha = .05$, test for any significant effects from factor A, factor B, or an interaction between the two factors.

Step 1: State the three null hypotheses for the given problem.

Step 2: Load the SAS software, and activate the PROGRAM EDITOR window.

Step 3: Type in your own SAS program for this two-factor factorial design, and submit the SAS program to run. You need to check the LOG window for errors.

> ➤ Notice that factor A has four levels while factor B has three levels. There are three replications for each cell.

Step 4: Print the SAS output, save the SAS program, and exit the SAS session.

Step 5: Summarize the results from the SAS output in an ANOVA table. Interpret the results on the main effects and the interaction.

Answer

The F value for factor A is 7.11, with 3 numerator degrees of freedom and 24 denominator degrees of freedom. Its p-value is .0014, which is less than α. Hence, factor A has a significant effect.

The F value for factor B is 1.32, with 2 numerator degrees of freedom and 24 denominator degrees of freedom. Its p-value is .2853, which exceeds α. Thus, factor B is not significant.

The F value for the interaction is 9.24, with 6 numerator degrees of freedom and 24 denominator degrees of freedom. Its p-value is .0001, which is less than α. Hence, the interaction also appears to have significant effects.

ASSIGNMENT 8

Correlation

OBJECTIVES

To examine the correlation between two variables using PROC CORR

To interpret the results from the SAS output

WHAT IS CORRELATION?

Researchers are often interested in quantifying the relationship between two variables. One way to do this is to measure the *correlation* between the two variables. Correlation is a measure of association that indicates both the strength of the relationship (for example, strong, moderate, or weak) and the direction of the relationship (for example, positive or negative) between two variables.

For example, let variable X be the daily umbrella sales figures in Boston and variable Y be the daily attendance figures for baseball games at Fenway Park in Boston. An interested observer would note that as umbrella sales (X) increase, the daily attendance figures (Y) tend to decrease. Thus, we would say that umbrella sales and baseball attendance are negatively correlated (as one goes up, the other tends to go down). However, we must be careful not to confuse correlation with causation. Clearly, an increase in umbrella sales does not *cause* the decrease in attendance. Rather, both are presumably results of an increase in rain.

The Pearson correlation coefficient measures the strength of association between two variables. However, before finding this correlation coefficient, it is often helpful, in the spirit of exploratory data analysis, to look at scatter plots of the variables.

AN EXAMPLE USING PROC CORR

Let's do an example. An investigator has collected IQ scores from eight pairs of identical twins (Twin A and Twin B) and wants to determine the correlation between the scores. What do you think the correlation between the twins' IQ scores would be? To find out, let's write a simple SAS program. Type in the following in the PROGRAM EDITOR window:

```
data iqscores;
input twina twinb @@;
cards;

106 115 127 117 85 89 73 61
102 98 85 100 97 98 110 108
;

proc plot;
plot twina*twinb;
run;

proc corr;
var twina twinb;
run;
```

The DATA step needs no elucidation, as you should be familiar by now with how to create a data set.

The first procedure is

```
proc plot;
```

which is used to generate various text-based plots of your data:

```
plot twina*twinb;
run;
```

Here, we are asking the computer for a *scatter plot* of the IQ scores for Twin A and the IQ scores of Twin B for each of the eight pairs of twins. The first variable named in the PLOT command will be measured along the *Y* (vertical) axis in the resulting plot; the second variable will be measured along the *X* (horizontal) axis.

The second procedure is

```
proc corr;
```

which calculates the Pearson correlation coefficient between the variables in your data.

The VAR statement

```
var twina twinb;
run;
```

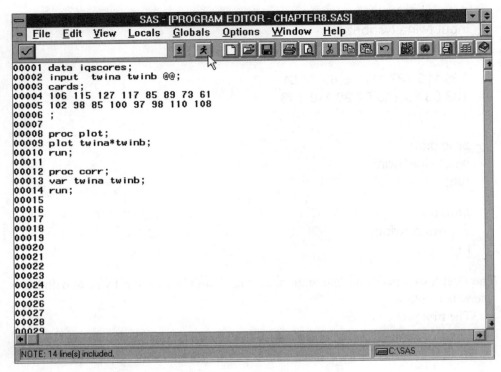

FIGURE 8.1   The Program for Correlation Analysis

tells the computer which variables to compute the correlation between. This is useful if you have more than two variables in your data set. Once you type your program, submit it, as in Figure 8.1.

INTERPRETING THE OUTPUT

After checking for errors, examine the output (click on **Window/OUTPUT**). Page one of the output (Figure 8.2) shows the scatter plot of the IQ scores for each pair of twins. Each **A** represents a pair of twins, with the IQ score of Twin A on the *Y* axis and the IQ score of Twin B on the *X* axis.

As you can see, there seems to be a positive relationship between these two variables. That is, IQ scores for the twins seem to be *positively correlated*. The slope of the trend of IQ scores is positive. The interpretation of positively correlated data is that as the IQ scores of Twin B (the *X* values) increase, the IQ scores of Twin A (the *Y* values) also tend to increase. If we encounter negatively correlated

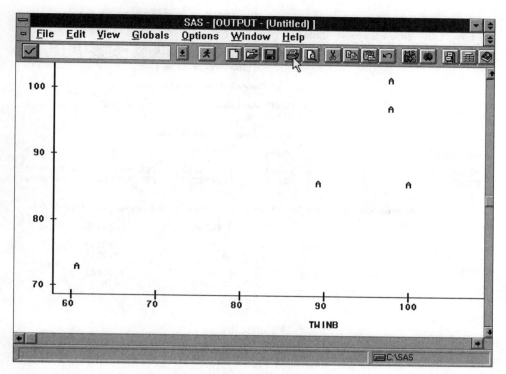

FIGURE 8.2   The Scatter Plot of the Twins Data

data, the slope of the trend would be downward. The interpretation would be that as the *X* values increase, the *Y* values tend to decrease.

Finally, examine page two of the output, which contains the results from PROC CORR (Figure 8.3). Descriptive statistics of the two variables are given, including the mean, standard deviation, sum, minimum, and maximum. Below these are the Pearson correlation coefficients. The correlation coefficient between the variables High and Low is 0.86207; that is, the twins' IQ scores are indeed positively correlated, as we indicated earlier.

Note that the correlation between Twina and Twinb is the same as the correlation between Twinb and Twina. Also note that the correlation between any variable and itself is 1. Finally, the SAS software provides the *p*-values of hypothesis tests checking whether the true correlation coefficients differ from zero. Small *p*-values indicate that the true correlation coefficient does indeed differ from zero. The *p*-value of 0.0059 is quite small, which is evidence that the twins' IQ scores are correlated.

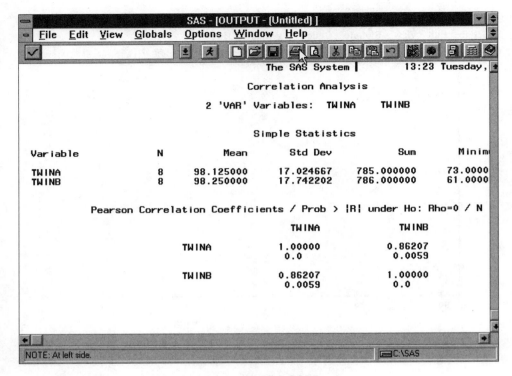

FIGURE 8.3   The Correlation Results from PROC CORR

ON YOUR OWN

Hands-On Exercise 8: Correlation

To better learn how to do correlation analysis, you should perform the following tasks step-by-step.

Suppose you are a psychologist who has developed a new intelligence test. As a measure of the test's reliability, you would like to see if the test yields about the same score every time it is administered. That is, you would like to explore whether different test scores from an individual subject are correlated. Here are the results from 12 individuals, who each took the test twice within three weeks. S# stands for the subject number, while T1 and T2 stand for the subjects' scores on each of the two tests.

S#	1	2	3	4	5	6	7	8	9	10	11	12
T1	3	22	19	18	15	10	11	13	7	6	20	18
T2	5	17	21	16	17	8	12	15	9	4	22	10

Using a scatter plot and correlation analysis, determine whether, and to what extent, the two test scores are correlated.

Step 1: Peruse the data set. Do high scores on Test 1 seem to be associated with high or low scores on Test 2? This should give you a preliminary idea concerning their correlation.

Step 2: Load the SAS software, and activate the PROGRAM EDITOR window.

Step 3: Type in your own SAS program to generate a scatter plot of the Test 2 versus the Test 1 scores. Also have your program produce the correlation coefficient for the test scores. Submit your program, and check the LOG window for errors.

Step 4: Print the SAS output, save the SAS program, and exit the SAS session.

Step 5: Interpret your output.
➤ Examine the scatter plots. Look for a pattern. Ask yourself: "As the Test 1 scores increase, do the Test 2 scores tend to go up or down?" This tells you that the data are positively or negatively correlated.
➤ Examine the PROC CORR results. What is the correlation coefficient between the test scores? Does this agree with your assessment from the scatter plots?

Answer

Perusal of the data set seems to indicate that high scores on Test 1 are associated with high scores on Test 2. This is supported by the scatter plot of the Test 2 scores against the Test 1 scores, which shows an increasing slope, indicating positive correlation. That is, as the Test 1 scores increase, the Test 2 scores tend to increase. Finally, the correlation coefficient for the test scores is 0.847, which indicates that the Test 1 scores are highly positively correlated with the Test 2 scores.

ASSIGNMENT 9

Linear Regression

OBJECTIVES

To perform regression using PROC REG

To interpret the results from the SAS output

HOW TO USE PROC REG TO PERFORM REGRESSION

In Assignment 8, you learned how to quantify the correlation between two variables. In this assignment, you will learn *linear regression*, which allows you to explore more fully the relationship between two quantitative variables.

In regression analysis, we use the *simple linear regression* model, which takes the form

$$Y = a + bX + e$$

where Y is the response or dependent variable, X is the independent or explanatory variable, a is the intercept constant, b is the slope coefficient, and e is the error term. When there is more than one independent variable, we should use a multiple regression model, but we will not discuss it in this handbook. Regression analysis uses the method of least squares to determine the values for a and b that provide the "best linear fit" for describing the relationship between the two variables. The equation that describes how the mean value of Y is related to X is called the *regression equation* and takes the form

$$E(Y) = a + bX$$

One way to perform regression analysis is to use PROC REG. The basic SAS command syntax to use PROC REG for simple linear regression is

```
PROC reg;
MODEL dependent variable = explanatory variable;
```

The PROC REG statement calls up the SAS regression analysis procedures. The MODEL statement is somewhat similar to the MODEL statements from Assignments 6 and 7. Notice, however, that there are no CLASS statements and no class variables.

AN EXAMPLE USING PROC REG

Let's do an example. Suppose you are interested in quantifying the relationship between the exam score (Y) and the number of hours spent studying (X) for a particular exam. Notice that the dependence in this relationship goes only one way. We would not want to say that the number of hours spent studying depended on the exam score (although the number of hours spent studying for the next test could!); rather, the score for this exam presumably depends on the time spent studying for it. We would like to determine if a linear relationship exists between these two variables and, if so, to quantify it.

To do this, we can first explore the relationship using a scatter plot. Then we need to quantify the strength and direction of this relationship by finding the correlation coefficient. Finally, we can more fully describe the linear aspect of the relationship using regression analysis.

Type the following program in the PROGRAM EDITOR:

```
data exam;
input hours score @@;
cards;

28 95 25 95 3 58 10 75 0 44
15 83 20 91 24 87 7 65 8 70
;

proc plot;
plot score*hours;
run;

proc corr;
var score hours;
run;

proc reg;
model score = hours;
run;
```

When the program is typed in, submit it, as in Figure 9.1.

INTERPRETING THE OUTPUT

After checking for errors (click on **Window/LOG**), examine the output (click on **Window/OUTPUT**). On page one of the output, the scatter plot of hours (Y)

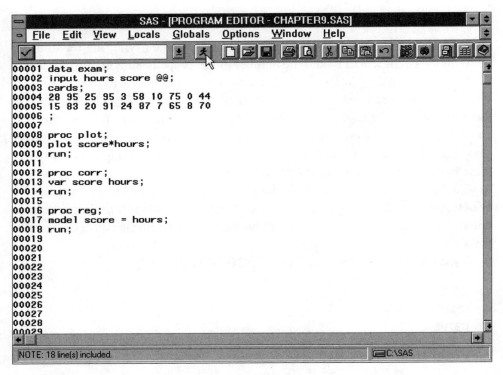

```
00001 data exam;
00002 input hours score @@;
00003 cards;
00004 28 95 25 95 3 58 10 75 0 44
00005 15 83 20 91 24 87 7 65 8 70
00006 ;
00007
00008 proc plot;
00009 plot score*hours;
00010 run;
00011
00012 proc corr;
00013 var score hours;
00014 run;
00015
00016 proc reg;
00017 model score = hours;
00018 run;
00019
00020
00021
00022
00023
00024
00025
00026
00027
00028
00029
```

FIGURE 9.1   The Program for Regression Analysis

against score (X) shows that as the number of hours spent studying increases, the exam score also tends to increase. We need to say "tends" because the relationship is not perfect, as indicated by careful examination of the plot. In one case, more time spent studying (24 compared to 20 hours) led to a decrease in exam score (87 compared to 91). However, this is an isolated instance, and the clear trend of the data is positive. The relationship is indeed positive and very strong, as indicated by the Pearson correlation coefficient of 0.95562 on page two of the output. Exam score and number of hours spent studying are highly positively correlated.

The regression results begin on page three of the output (Figure 9.2). The ANOVA table is given, which concisely presents various regression results. The *total sum of squares* represents the total amount of variability in the response data (*Y*: exam score). The *model sum of squares* is the amount of this variability that is explained by the regression equation, that is, by the relationship between hours and score. The ratio of model sum of squares to total sum of squares is the famous *R*-squared, which is an indication of the goodness-of-fit of the regression. Here,

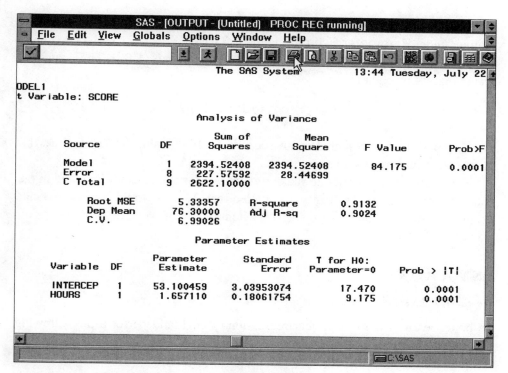

FIGURE 9.2   The Regression Results from PROC REG

our *R*-squared is 0.9132, which indicates that the number of hours spent studying explains about 91% of the variability in exam score. This is very high, but it might be improved if we examined further models or introduced more explanatory variables. Another important statistic is the *p*-value for the regression (model) as a whole. Small *p*-values indicate a significant relationship between the variables. Here, our *p*-value (shown as Prob > F in the ANOVA table) of 0.0001 is very small—strong evidence that exam score has a significant relationship with hours spent studying. The standard error of the estimate *e* is 5.33357, which can be used to develop the confidence interval of $E(Y)$ and the prediction interval of Y_p.

As can be seen in Figure 9.2, the output also provides results of *t* tests for the two parameters *a* (INTERCEP) and *b* (HOURS). You can consult your statistics instructor for further details.

Finally, once we accept the significance of the relationship, the *estimated regression equation*

$$\hat{Y} = \hat{a} + \hat{b}X$$

quantifies this relationship. Look at the output under **Parameter Estimates**. The number under **Parameter Estimate** in the **INTERCEP** row is a (53.1); the number under **Parameter Estimate** in the **HOURS** row is b (1.66). Thus, our estimated regression equation is

$$\hat{Y} = 53.100459 + 1.657110X$$

In other words, the estimated exam score is 53.10459 plus 1.657110 times the number of hours spent studying.

We can use this equation to make predictions for students not included in our data set. For example, a student who studied for 12 hours would have a predicted exam score of: $53.100459 + 1.657110 (12 \text{ hours}) = 72.9856$.

ON YOUR OWN

Hands-On Exercise 9: Linear Regression

To better learn how to use linear regression, you should perform the following tasks step-by-step.

Suppose you are investigating the relationship between mathematics anxiety and statistics performance. You administer a math anxiety scale to 12 statistics students and compare the results to their scores on their first stats quiz. Use a scatter plot, correlation analysis, and regression analysis to determine whether a relationship exists between math anxiety and statistics performance, and describe what kind of relationship it is. Here are the data; let the math anxiety scores (ma) be the dependent variable (y) and the quiz scores (q) be the independent variable (x); st. stands for the individual student.

st.	1	2	3	4	5	6	7	8	9	10	11	12
ma	2	13	12	10	8	3	7	6	9	10	4	7
q	10	3	4	6	8	10	5	10	6	2	8	5

Step 1: Peruse the data set. Do high math anxiety scores seem to be associated with high statistics quiz scores or with low scores? This should give you a preliminary idea concerning their correlation.

Step 2: Load the SAS software, and activate the PROGRAM EDITOR window.

Step 3: Type in your own SAS program to generate a scatter plot of the statistics test scores versus the math anxiety scores. Also have your program produce the correlation coefficient for these variables. Finally, have the program run a regression of the statistics quiz scores (y) against the math anxiety scores (x). Submit your program, and check the LOG window for errors.

Step 4:   Print the SAS output, save your SAS program, and exit the SAS session.

Step 5:   Interpret your output.

➤   Examine the scatter plots. Look for a pattern. Ask yourself: "As the math anxiety scores increase, do the statistics quiz scores tend to go up or down?" This tells you that the data are positively or negatively correlated.

➤   Examine the PROC CORR results. What is the correlation coefficient between the test scores? Does this agree with your assessment from the scatter plots?

➤   Examine the regression results. Is the regression significant? That is, is the p-value small enough to show evidence of a relationship between math anxiety and statistics quiz performance? What is the R-squared? That is, how much of the variation in the statistics quiz scores is explained by the relationship with the math anxiety scores? What is the estimated regression equation? That is, what are the values of the slope (b) and intercept (a) of the regression line? Finally, make a prediction of a new student's statistics quiz score if she had a math anxiety score of 5.

Answer

Perusal of the data set seems to indicate that high math anxiety scores are associated with low statistics quiz scores. This is supported by the scatter plot, which shows a decreasing slope, indicating negative correlation. That is, as math anxiety scores increase, statistics quiz scores tend to decrease.

From the correlation analysis results, we find that the correlation coefficient for these variables is –0.82435, which indicates numerically that the math anxiety scores are strongly negatively correlated with the statistics quiz scores.

Finally, we examine the regression analysis results. The small p-value (Prob > F) of .0010 is evidence of a relationship between our two variables of interest. The R-squared of 0.6795 indicates that about two-thirds of the variability in the statistics quiz scores is explained by their relationship with the math anxiety scores. The estimated regression equation is:

The estimated statistics quiz score equals 11.451305 minus 0.663908 times the math anxiety score.

(Note the *minus* because of the negative sign for the slope.) Therefore, for the new student with a math anxiety score of 5, we would predict her statistics quiz score to be $11.451305 - 0.663908(5) = 8.131405$. That is, her low math anxiety score led to a prediction of a high statistics quiz score.

ASSIGNMENT 10

Chi-Square Tests of Goodness-of-Fit and Independence

OBJECTIVES

To perform a Chi-square test for the goodness-of-fit

To perform a Chi-square test for independence using contingency tables

---

In this assignment, we are concerned with the case in which each observation in the data set is assigned to exactly one of several mutually exclusive "cells" or categories. This kind of data is usually called *categorical data*. The statistical problem is to test whether the observed category frequencies tend to be close to those expected category frequencies when the stated null hypothesis is true. We consider two hypothesis-testing problems here in particular, both based on the use of the Chi-square distribution:

1. A goodness-of-fit test for a multinomial population
2. A test for independence using contingency tables

In this assignment, you will learn first how to perform a Chi-square test for the goodness-of-fit and then how to run a Chi-square test for independence using contingency tables.

HOW TO PERFORM A CHI-SQUARE TEST FOR THE GOODNESS-OF-FIT

The purpose of the Chi-square goodness-of-fit test is to test the null hypothesis that a given set of observations is drawn from, or "fits," a specified probability distribution. Here, we consider a general situation in which the hypothesized probability distribution is a multinomial distribution. The multinomial distribution can be thought of as an extension of the binomial distribution to the case of three or more categories.

For example, a statistics professor has taught a statistics course for several years and has found that the student grade distribution in the course has consistently been as follows: 10% A, 20% B, 35% C, 25% D, and 10% F. A sample of 80 statistics grades at the end of this semester showed 5 A's, 22 B's, 25 C's, 18 D's, and 10 F's. Using $\alpha = .05$, test the claim that the student grades this semester have the same distribution as in the past. In this example, the population of interest is a multinomial distribution; each actual statistics grade can be classified into one of five categories: A, B, C, D, and F. Let us define the following notation:

p_A = proportion of actual A grades

p_B = proportion of actual B grades

p_C = proportion of actual C grades

p_D = proportion of actual D grades

p_E = proportion of actual F grades

To test whether the actual grades have the same distribution as in the past, we establish the following null and alternative hypotheses:

H_0: $p_A = .10, p_B = .20, p_C = .35, p_D = .25,$ and $p_F = .10$

H_a: The population proportions are not
$p_A = .10, p_B = .20, p_C = .35, p_D = .25,$ and $p_F = .10$

Note that H_a does not require all of the proportions to differ from those in H_0. If the null hypothesis H_0 is true, then the theoretical expected frequency for each of five categories can be obtained by multiplying the sample size $n = 80$ by the hypothesized proportion for the category. The observed frequencies and expected frequencies are summarized in the following table

Category	A Grades	B Grades	C Grades	D Grades	F Grades
Observed frequency (O_i)	5	22	25	18	10
Expected frequency (E_i)	8	16	28	20	8

The Chi-square test statistic is computed by

$$\chi^2 = \sum_{i=1}^{k} \frac{(O_i - E_i)^2}{E_i}$$

where k is the number of mutually exclusive categories involved. The test statistic has a Chi-square distribution with $k - 1$ degrees of freedom provided that the expected frequencies are 5 or more for all categories. As our table shows, the expected frequencies are all 5 or more, so we can use the SAS software to proceed with the computation of χ^2.

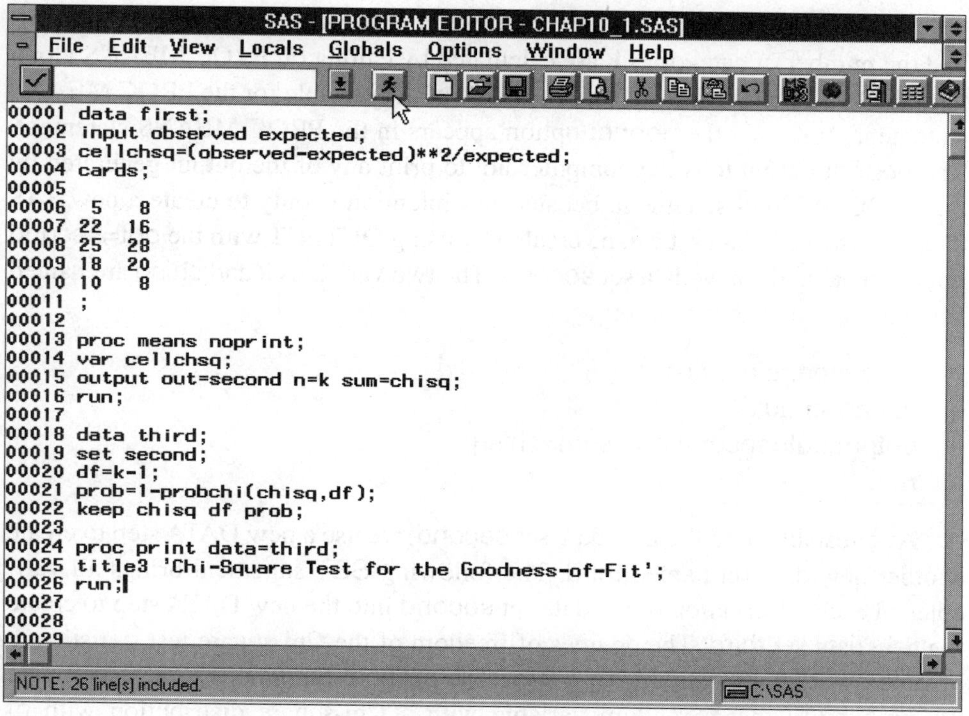

```
00001 data first;
00002 input observed expected;
00003 cellchsq=(observed-expected)**2/expected;
00004 cards;
00005
00006  5   8
00007 22  16
00008 25  28
00009 18  20
00010 10   8
00011 ;
00012
00013 proc means noprint;
00014 var cellchsq;
00015 output out=second n=k sum=chisq;
00016 run;
00017
00018 data third;
00019 set second;
00020 df=k-1;
00021 prob=1-probchi(chisq,df);
00022 keep chisq df prob;
00023
00024 proc print data=third;
00025 title3 'Chi-Square Test for the Goodness-of-Fit';
00026 run;
00027
00028
00029
```

FIGURE 10.1 The Program for the Chi-Square Test for Goodness-of-Fit

Now we need to launch SAS for Windows and type in a SAS example program in the PROGRAM EDITOR window (Figure 10.1). However, for the Chi-square goodness-of-fit test, the SAS software does not have a simple procedure. The method introduced here is to write a SAS program that uses the MEANS procedure, the probchi (probability of Chi-square) function, and the Print procedure.

Now let's examine the SAS code used for this problem. In the first DATA step of the program, we create a data set called first and input two variables, observed (observed frequency) and expected (expected frequency). Then we create the new variable cellchsq that equals (observed–expected)**2/expected for each category, as in the formula for the χ^2 statistic. The data sets of both observed and expected frequencies are entered after the CARDS statement:

```
data first;
input observed expected;
cellchsq=(observed–expected)**2/expected;
cards;
```

The summation of the variable cellchsq for all categories named chisq (χ^2) and the number of categories k are calculated by calling on PROC MEANS along with the VAR statement to specify the name of the variable for the PROC MEANS statement. Note that the noprint option appears in the PROC MEANS statement. The noprint option tells the computer not to print any of the output generated by the PROC MEANS statement, because our intention is only to create a new SAS data set. The new data set can be created by using OUTPUT with the out=second option to name the new data set second. The two variables k and chisq are named and output to this new data set:

```
proc means noprint;
var cellchsq;
output out=second n=k sum=chisq;
run;
```

After establishing the new data set second, we use a new DATA step to create another new data set named third. The following SET statement brings all variables in each observation of the data set second into the new DATA step to create the new data set third. The degrees of freedom of the Chi-square test statistic are obtained by the new variable df = k−1. The probchi function is used to compute the probability that a random variable with a Chi-square distribution with df degrees of freedom falls below the given chisq value. The variable prob gives the p-value of the Chi-square test statistic. The KEEP statement specifies the variables chisq, df, and prob that we want to retain in the data set third. The KEEP statement can appear anywhere among the program statements in the DATA step.

```
data third;
set second;
df=k−1;
prob=1−probchi(chisq,df);
keep chisq df prob;
```

Finally, a summary of the variables chisq, df, and prob will be displayed in the OUTPUT window by calling on PROC PRINT. The data=third option tells the computer that the new data set third is to be used by the PROC PRINT statement. The title3 statement tells the computer that the title Chi-Square Test for the Goodness-of-Fit will print on the third line of output.

```
proc print data=third;
title3 'Chi-Square Test for the Goodness-of-Fit';
run;
```

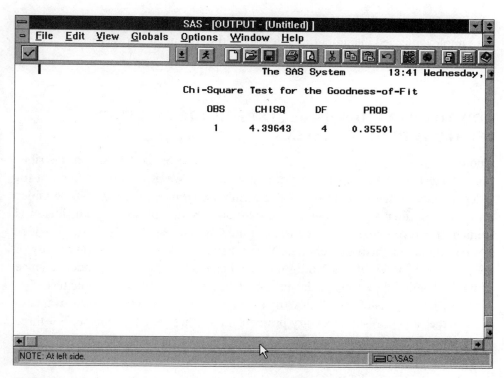

FIGURE 10.2   The Output from the Chi-Square Test for Goodness-of-Fit

After we submit the SAS program, we can see the results of the Chi-square test in the OUTPUT window (Figure 10.2). The test statistic χ^2 is **4.39643**, with **4** degrees of freedom, and is used to test the null hypothesis:

$$H_0:\; p_A = .10,\, p_B = .20,\, p_C = .35,\, p_D = .25,\, p_F = .10$$

The p-value associated with this test statistic is **0.35501**, which is larger than $\alpha = .05$; thus, the null hypothesis H_0 *cannot* be rejected. The evidence supports the hypothesis that the student grades this semester have the same distribution as in the past.

Notice that the Chi-square goodness-of-fit test can generally be used with any hypothesized probability distribution (a Poisson or a normal probability distribution, for instance). The test procedure introduced here still follows so long as you establish k mutually exclusive categories of sample data and find corresponding observed and expected frequencies for all categories, provided that all expected frequencies are 5 or more. The only change needed is that the degrees of freedom of the Chi-square test statistic become $df = k - 1 - m$, where m is the number of unknown parameters of the hypothesized probability distribution estimated from the sample data used in computing the expected frequencies. However, we will not discuss the details of these situations.

HOW TO RUN A CHI-SQUARE TEST FOR INDEPENDENCE USING CONTINGENCY TABLES

Another hypothesis-testing problem based on the use of the Chi-square distribution is to test for the independence of two variables. We now illustrate the test for independence in the context of what are called *contingency tables*. These tables arise in experiments where one of the two random variables being considered is studied at r levels and the other is examined at c levels. This usually provides $r \times c$ mutually exclusive categories. The statistical analysis is based on a study of the number of observations falling into each category. The test for independence using the contingency table is also called a Chi-square contingency table test.

Now let us consider the following example. A psychology professor wants to see whether algebra is a necessary prerequisite for her statistics course. For three semesters, she records the number of students passing, failing, or dropping the course as a function of whether they have had college algebra. The following contingency table shows her data:

	Pass	Fail	Drop
Algebra	25	5	5
No algebra	12	14	8

Using $\alpha = .01$, test that the number of students passing, failing, or dropping the course is independent of whether the student had college algebra.

To test for independence by using the preceding 2×3 contingency table, we establish the following null and alternative hypothesis:

H_0: The number of students passing, failing, or dropping the course is independent of whether the student had college algebra.

H_a: The number of students passing, failing, or dropping the course is *not* independent of whether the student had college algebra.

The Chi-square test for independence using a contingency table can be performed by calling on the freq procedure with a special data input format in the DATA step using the DO and END statements. Thus, we do not need to figure out the expected frequency for each of the contingency table categories by ourselves.

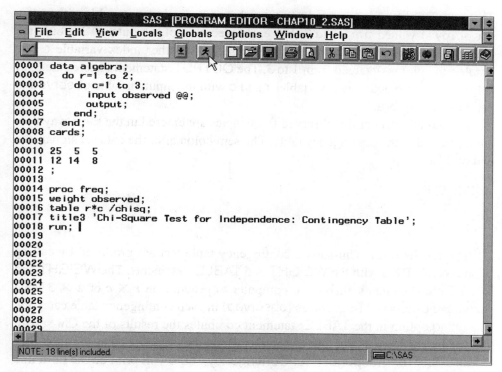

FIGURE 10.3   The Program for the Chi-Square Test for Independence

Let us launch SAS for Windows once again and then type in a new SAS example program in the PROGRAM EDITOR window (Figure 10.3). In the DATA step of the example program, we create a data set named **algebra** and define a variable **observed** (observed frequency) by using the INPUT statement. The @@ symbol tells the computer that there will be more than one observation entered per line in the data set after the CARDS statement. The new statements used here are the DO and the END statements. The statements between the DO and the END are called a *DO group*. An END statement must end every DO group in the SAS program.

```
data algebra;
  do r=1 to 2;
    do c=1 to 3;
      input observed @@;
      output;
    end;
  end;
cards;
```

The outer DO group is executed two times based on the index variable r (the number of rows) valued from 1 to 2. For each execution of the outer DO group, the inner DO group is executed three times based on another index variable c (the number of columns) valued from 1 to 3. The OUTPUT statement enables the SAS software to write both index variables r and c with the input variable observed to the data set algebra.

The sample data or the observed frequencies are entered in the same way they are displayed in the contingency table. The semicolon after the data set signals the end of data.

```
25 5 5
12 14 8
;
```

The results of the Chi-square contingency table test are produced by calling upon PROC FREQ with the WEIGHT and TABLE statements. The WEIGHT and TABLE r*c statements enable the computer to produce an $r \times c$ or 2×3 table showing the observed frequencies (observed) in each contingency table category. The chisq option in the TABLE statement computes the results of the Chi-square test for independence. The title3 statement tells the computer that the title Chi-Square Test for Independence: Contingency Table will print on the third line of output.

```
proc freq;
weight observed;
table r*c / chisq;
title3 'Chi-Square Test for Independence: Contingency Table';
run;
```

To obtain the SAS output, we must submit the SAS program for execution. The results of the Chi-square test for independence are then displayed in the OUTPUT window (Figure 10.4). You need to scroll the window down using the vertical scrollbar at the right to get a complete look at the SAS output. In the table output, the observed frequency, percent, row percent, and column percent are summarized for every contingency table category. The row and column totals are also reported for the contingency table. In the statistics output, the Chi-square test statistic χ^2 is 9.511, with 3 degrees of freedom, and it is used to test for independence. The p-value of the test statistic is 0.009 under Prob. We know that the p-value is less than $\alpha = .01$; thus, the null hypothesis H_0 is rejected. Therefore, we conclude that the number of students passing, failing, or dropping the course is not independent of whether the student had college algebra.

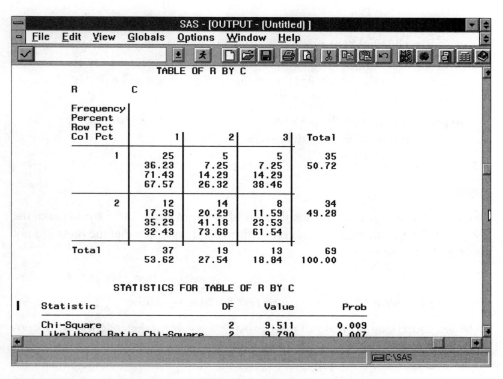

FIGURE 10.4   The Output from the Chi-Square Test for Independence

ON YOUR OWN

Hands-On Exercise 10.1: Chi-Square Test for the Goodness-of-Fit

To better learn how to run the Chi-square test for the goodness-of-fit, you should perform the following tasks step-by-step.

Children were fed one of four different diets for a week and then were tested for their ability to solve complex word problems. There were four diet groups, and the total number of problems solved in each group was as follows: Diet A, 43; Diet B, 57; Diet C, 50; Diet D, 40. Using the 5% level of significance, test to see whether the diets had any significant effect on problem solving.

Step 1:   State the null and alternative hypotheses for the given problem.

Step 2:   Compute the expected frequency E_i for each category.
➤   Make sure each E_i is larger than or equal to 5.

Step 3:   Load the SAS software, and activate the PROGRAM EDITOR window.

Step 4:   Type in your own SAS program for this goodness-of-fit test problem, and then submit the SAS program to run. You need to check the LOG window for errors.

Step 5:   Print the SAS output, save the SAS program, and exit the SAS session.

Step 6:   Summarize the SAS output, and draw the conclusion for the problem. What is the *p*-value of the test?

Answer

The test statistic χ^2 is 3.64211, the degrees of freedom are 3, and the *p*-value of the test is .30279. Fail to reject the null hypothesis and conclude that the diets did not affect problem solving.

Hands-On Exercise 10.2: Chi-Square Test for Independence

To better understand how to run the Chi-square test for independence using contingency tables, you should perform the following tasks step-by-step.

In a study of the relationship between early childhood trauma and adjustment to school, a school psychologist classified students according to whether they had a history of trauma (for example, severe illness, death of a parent) and by their adjustment to school. The data are given below.

| | *Adjustment* | | |
	Poor	Average	Excellent
No trauma	16	30	50
Trauma	14	6	4

Using $\alpha = .05$, test to determine whether trauma affects adjustment to school.

Step 1:   State the null and alternative hypotheses for the given problem. Count the number of rows and the number of columns in the contingency table.

Step 2:   Load the SAS software, and activate the PROGRAM EDITOR window.

Step 3:   Type in your own SAS program for this Chi-square test for independence problem, and then submit the SAS program to run. You need to check the LOG window for errors.

Step 4: Print the SAS output, save the SAS program, and exit the SAS session.

Step 5: Summarize the SAS output, and draw the conclusion for the problem. What is the p-value of the test?

Answer

The test statistic χ^2 is 18.935, the degrees of freedom are 2, and the p-value of the test is .001. Reject the null hypothesis and conclude that students with a history of trauma were more likely to have poor adjustment to school.

Appendix: Troubleshooting

Do not be distressed if your program doesn't run the first time. This happens so often, at all levels of computer programming, that professional programmers have coined a term for it: *debugging*. Fortunately, many of the problems that stop our SAS programs from running stem from a relatively small number of errors.

Q. My program won't run. When I look in the log file, it says something like:

ERROR 180-322: Statement is not valid or it is used out of
proper order.

What's wrong?

A. This is a very common type of error message. It is usually caused by one of three things. First, you may have forgotten a semicolon (;). Second, you may have misspelled a command. Third, you may have used a command incorrectly or out of order.

It is a good idea to make 100% sure that *every* SAS line (except where the data is input) ends in a semicolon. Check every line of your program in the PROGRAM EDITOR window (click on **Window/PROGRAM EDITOR** and then **Locals/ Recall text**). Be meticulous. If you find a line that is missing a semicolon, put it in and re-submit the program. If all your semicolons are present, try the next step.

Perhaps you misspelled a command. For example, if you spell the **CARDS** statement as *CAS*, the SAS software will not understand and report the error in the LOG. Nevertheless, SAS software is quite clever and will catch many misspellings. For example, if you misspell **INPUT** as *INPT*, your program will run and you may receive the following warning in the LOG:

WARNING 1-322: Assuming the symbol INPUT was misspelled
as INPT.

If all your commands are spelled right, then the error is most likely caused by a statement that is actually invalid or out of proper order, as the message indicates. Make sure that your command belongs with the type of analysis you are doing. Check that you are not using commands from some other statistical package, such as Minitab.

SAS software is rather picky about the ordering of commands. For example, in the DATA step, if you have the **CARDS** command ahead of the **INPUT** command, the computer will give you an error message about being out of proper order. Go back to the program and make sure all your commands are in the proper order. If appropriate, compare them with the examples in the handbook.

Q. The OUTPUT window says that I have only 1 observation in the data set, but I know that I input all 10 observations. What's wrong?

A. The reason the SAS software is seeing only 1 observation may be that you may have forgotten to put @ @ after the variables in the input statement. Try it and see.

Q. There is no output from my program. My data set is named example. When I look at the LOG window, it gives me an error message that says:

ERROR: File WORK.EXAMPLE1.DATA does not exist.

A. Often, this error is caused by misspelling a reference to a data set that has already been created. In this instance, the data set named example was misspelled in a reference to it later in the program (for example, proc print data = example1).

Q. When I print out the output, I get many more pages than I want, including old stuff that I ran earlier today. What do I do?

A. The OUTPUT window and the SAS log accumulate materials from your entire SAS session. Usually, you don't want to print out all that old stuff. So go to the OUTPUT window and click on Edit/Clear text; then do the same in the SAS log. Then run your program one last time and print it out.

Q. I closed the PROGRAM EDITOR window by mistake, and now I can't type in my program. What do I do?

A. Click on Globals/PROGRAM EDITOR and type away. The same goes for when you close the other windows.

Q. I would like to explore some sample programs that other people have written. Maybe they could give me some ideas. How do I do this?

A. Click on Help/Sample programs. Then choose your category.

Q. I am ready to learn more about statistical analysis in SAS for Windows. What can I do?

A. One thing you can do is access the extensive online training that is available in SAS for Windows. Also, you can find a wealth of information on the World Wide Web. See the References for further information.

References

Mayfield Publishing Company Statistics Resources

Thorne, B. M., and Slane, S. (1987). *Statistics for the behavioral sciences* (2nd ed.). Mountain View, CA: Mayfield.

Pavkov, T. W., and Pierce, K. A. (1998). *Ready, set, go! A student guide to SPSS® for Windows 7.5®*. Mountain View, CA: Mayfield.

SAS Resources

If you have further questions about SAS software or SAS for Windows, or if you would like to learn more about this powerful statistical package, here are some resources.

Books

SAS Institute. (1985). *SAS user's guide: Basics and SAS user's guide, statistics.* Cary, NC: SAS Institute Inc.

The SAS Institute is the source of a great wealth of information about SAS software, including various manuals examining every conceivable option.

Shin, K. (1994). *SAS guide.* Boston: Irwin. Published as part of the Irwin Statistical Software Series.

This useful guide contains many helpful examples for DOS SAS that can readily be translated for SAS for Windows.

Web Sites

This is the home page of the SAS Institute itself:
http://www.sas.com/

This site from York University in Toronto gives an overview of SAS:
http://www.yorku.ca/dept/psych/lab/sas/sasprog.htm

This site, also from York University, takes a look at SAS for Windows:
http://www.yorku.ca/dept/psych/lab/sas/sas4win.htm

This site from the University of Texas helps you get started with SAS for Windows:
http://www.utexas.edu/cc/docs/stat47.html

This site from Indiana University is a primer for getting started with SAS for Windows:

http://www.indiana.edu/~statmath/smdoc/saswin.html

This site from Cornell University answers frequently asked questions about SAS software:

http://www.ciser.cornell.edu/FAQ/SAS.html

Data Set Sites

Looking for data to analyze? You will find all you want, and more, at these sites.

From York University in Toronto:

http://www.math.yorku.ca/SCS/StatResource.html#Data

From the University of Nevada:

http://www.scs.unr.edu/~cbmr/research/data.html

From the University of Queensland, Australia:

http://www.maths.uq.oz.au/~gks/webguide/datasets.html

From Carnegie Mellon University:

http://lib.stat.cmu.edu/datasets/